T0277091

Brimming with creative inspiration, how-to projects, and useful information to enrich your everyday life, Quarto.com is a favorite destination for those pursuing their interests and passions.

Inspiring | Educating | Creating | Entertaining

© 2022 Quarto Publishing Group USA Inc.
Text © 2022 Kathy Jentz and Teresa Speight

First Published in 2022 by Cool Springs Press, an imprint of The Quarto Group,
100 Cummings Center, Suite 265-D, Beverly, MA 01915, USA.
T (978) 282-9590 F (978) 283-2742 Quarto.com

All rights reserved. No part of this book may be reproduced in any form without written permission of the copyright owners. All images in this book have been reproduced with the knowledge and prior consent of the artists concerned, and no responsibility is accepted by producer, publisher, or printer for any infringement of copyright or otherwise, arising from the contents of this publication. Every effort has been made to ensure that credits accurately comply with information supplied. We apologize for any inaccuracies that may have occurred and will resolve inaccurate or missing information in a subsequent reprinting of the book.

Cool Springs Press titles are also available at discount for retail, wholesale, promotional, and bulk purchase. For details, contact the Special Sales Manager by email at specialsales@quarto.com or by mail at The Quarto Group, Attn: Special Sales Manager, 100 Cummings Center, Suite 265-D, Beverly, MA 01915, USA.

26 25 24 23 22   1 2 3 4 5

ISBN: 978-0-7603-7301-9

Digital edition published in 2022
eISBN: 978-0-7603-7302-6

Library of Congress Cataloging-in-Publication Data

Jentz, Kathy, author. | Speight, Teri, author.
The urban garden : 101 ways to grow food and beauty in the city / Kathy Jentz, Teri Speight.
ISBN 9780760373019 (board) | ISBN 9780760373026 (ebook)
1. Urban gardening--Handbooks, manuals, etc. 2. Urban gardens. 3. Small gardens.
LCC SB454 .J56 2022 (print) | LCC SB454 (ebook) | DDC 635.09173/2--dc23/eng/20211001

LCCN 2021046559 (print) | LCCN 2021046560 (ebook)

Design and page layout: Laura Shaw Design
Front Cover Image: Alamy
Back Cover images: Shutterstock

Printed in China

THE **URBAN GARDEN**

101 Ways to Grow Food and Beauty in the City

KATHY JENTZ + TERI SPEIGHT

COOL
SPRINGS
PRESS

Contents

Introduction

All of us have limits. Whether it be the constraints on our personal time, budgets, or energy levels, there is a limit to how much we can personally garden. Small-space gardening is a fact of life for a majority of those living in urban neighborhoods and we often chafe against these boundaries, but as any good poet or artist will tell you, the permission to not have to tackle everything and focus on just one finite aspect of a topic is freeing. Because our urban spaces are limited, we don't need to worry about those big space choices like rotating fields of crops or maintaining an old-growth forest. Instead, we get to concentrate on creating tiny jewel boxes of perfection!

There are many creative ways to tackle urban gardening challenges. In this book, we'll take a look at clever methods for intensely gardening in tight areas, maximizing available growing spaces, and making the most of the benefits of raising plants in confined boundaries.

We also want you to be inspired by examples of beauty in urban gardens. This book is filled with images taken from cities all over the world that demonstrate how growing in constrained spots is not a limitation on creating a garden of beauty and bounty.

We are inspired by new and veteran gardeners who push the envelope of innovative ideas. The examples in this book are from our own decades of urban gardening experiences and gleaned from our pool of fellow green-thumb experts. Our goal is to encourage diversity by engaging those of you who are new to gardening and those who are already experienced urban gardeners.

You may have made some prior attempts at growing and have not been very successful at it. Don't let that discourage you. Here is a secret: All gardeners kill plants! That is how we learn. Each time we try is a chance to learn something new. The important thing is that we take note of what might have gone wrong, we adjust, and we try again. We hope that the examples and guidance in this book will help set you on the path of future success and continued learning.

Now, your green thumb is itching to get growing, but you don't have a big yard to dig into? Don't think a garden is out of reach! Instead, think creatively and explore the sunny outdoor spaces around your abode. Do you have access to a balcony, patio, or rooftop? How about a shared back alley or maybe you can rent an allotment plot? Growing spaces are all around you, once you start opening your eyes to them.

Sometimes the answer is a neglected green space that is in need of some TLC (tender loving care). Start asking around amongst your neighbors, coworkers, friends, and family. Many people have spaces to share that can be turned into gardens that they would be willing to lend for free or for a portion of the flowers or for some of the produce that you grow. Take that little step forward and ask!

Once you have carved out a bit of growing space foryourself, assess the growing conditions there. You will need to know the hardiness and heat zone, hours of sunlight, average rainfall, and any other factors that may impact plant health in your region. For example, is there an annual dry period? Are there prevailing winds? If you are growing in the ground, what is the texture and composition of the soil?

After you have determined these factors, you can start researching a plant list. This is where your personal tastes and ambitions come in. Maybe you love insects and animals and want an all-native garden to support local wildlife, or you love cooking and want to create the ultimate kitchen garden. Maybe you want a home and office filled with fresh bouquets of flowers that you have grown in your own garden from seed. Maybe you want to do all of these things! In the chapters ahead, we'll illustrate how to get started on those growing dreams—in the little spaces you have set aside to nurture them.

CHAPTER 1

Clever Containers

O PTIONS FOR PLANTING in containers have changed over time. In this chapter, we encourage you to think beyond the usual clay and ceramic pots. There are many new containers made from modern materials that will help the gardener in numerous ways. One example is self-watering pots to maintain hydration of the plant material. Another advantage is using moveable planters so you can have versatility in creating different planting combinations throughout the season.

Consider using alternative materials for a unique stackable container to plant a multitude of interesting plants. If you are short on space, there are even containers that are used for growing plants during the gardening season and then emptied and stored flat inside afterward. Thinking outside the box offers many options for creative containers.

Stock Tank Planters

Stock tank planters provide a large planting space above ground that is easily accessible for working in them, plus they are an attractive space divider or garden feature in and of themselves too. Originating in the country for use in raising livestock, stock tanks have now become urban chic. Some city-dwelling gardeners love gardening in stock tanks so much that they use them as their planting beds and barriers—creating a row of them as a divider between their neighbors' yards or back alleys.

The metal bottoms of stock tanks keep out burrowing rodents and they are tall enough to keep slugs and rabbits out as well. Stock tanks are also a great solution for locations where the soil might be contaminated with heavy metals or otherwise are unsuitable for planting directly into the ground.

Stock tanks come in various sizes and shapes—from short ones for sheep to taller ones for horses and cattle. Typically, they are made from galvanized steel and are fairly lightweight—that is until they are filled with soil, plants, and water. The bottoms are solid to hold in the water, therefore you will need to drill several drainage holes into them. Pour in landscape gravel to a depth of 6 inches (15 cm) and cover with landscape fabric or other material to keep the soil and plant roots in their own layer above the gravel.

Because they are metal stock tanks, they warm up quickly in the spring, so you can plant in them earlier than in the ground. If you live in a very hot climate, you can line the interior with insulation, cardboard, or carpeting so the soil doesn't get too hot.

Metal stock tanks can also dry out faster than other containers and need more frequent watering. You can install a simple drip-irrigation system to keep up with that aspect of maintenance.

The stock tanks are very adaptable and versatile. You can attach wheels on the bottom for greater mobility. You can also paint them as you like and add other decorations. Shorter tanks can be placed on bricks or other risers, as long as the base can handle the weight of the filled tank.

Because they are large and stable, you can add vertical elements to them such as tall poles and netting for trellises to train vines up them.

There is no limit to what you can plant in them from a vegetable garden to a pollinator habitat or any combination you might like to try!

Building Deeper Window Boxes

A well-made window box can add value to the simplest window. A deep window box allows the homeowner to create a planting abundantly filled with flowers. There are certain steps to take when building a window box that will help make it last for years.

Measuring the width of the window or windows accurately is the first and most important step. It is important to make any well-proportioned window box the exact width of the window.

Consider the depth of the box. When thinking about the different plants you might want to include, ensure your box has a minimum depth of at least 8 inches (20 cm). This will allow most plant roots to grow and thrive without being cramped.

Choose brackets that are sturdy but also complement the home and garden. Window boxes should blend in with the theme of the garden. A sturdy bracket needs to hold the window box, saturated soil, and plants—which can be quite heavy.

Average window boxes are 8 to 12 inches (20 to 30 cm) wide. The bracket should protrude a bit from the underside of the window box to adequately secure the weight of the wet soil and plants. Leave at least ¾ to 1 inch (2 to 2.5 cm) of airspace behind the window box to allow the air to circulate, preventing damage or rot of the house. Measure and mark where the brackets will best balance the window box. Then, install the appropriate anchor into the exterior of the house.

Creating a deeper window box requires careful consideration when selecting the materials. It is important to choose a rot-resistant wood or a faux wood. There are many lightweight and practical composites available that mimic wood and still look attractive.

Measure accurately and cut the pieces for the front, back, sides, and bottom. Make certain the bottom piece will accommodate the side pieces so they can be screwed in securely.

Assemble the box upside down. First create the frame by positioning and securing the front, sides, and back pieces with screws or nails. Make certain to secure these pieces together using hardware suitable for outdoors. Position the bottom piece on top of the frame and secure in place.

Using sandpaper smooth any rough edges. With a drill, add enough drainage holes on the bottom to allow the soil to drain freely. Usually, drainage holes are spaced approximately 12 inches (30 cm) apart. Measuring 6 inches (15 cm) in from the sides, mark the first drainage hole. Stagger the holes so the soil drains consistently. If you are considering painting or embellishing the window box, you want to do this prior to the final installation.

Choosing a solid color of paint is always safe. However, consider using a stencil or template to add a pattern or additional color(s) for eclectic flair. If attractive, it can become a work of art in itself—even when a window box is empty.

Make certain you have installed the brackets securely using an anchor. Depending on the length, three brackets may be used to ensure even distribution of the weight of the window box.

Add good quality container or potting soil, leaving 2 inches (5 cm) at the top of the window box to allow for watering. Deciding what to plant just might be the hardest part. Remember, the plants are the main attraction, and the window box is the stage.

Self-Watering Containers

In the heat of the summer, utilizing self-watering containers will keep potted plants hydrated. Instead of hand watering or using the hose daily, self-watering pots are an efficient way to ensure water is readily available. These types of pots come in handy as we work, travel, and have busy lifestyles. Consider all the options when selecting the right planter. Containers that take care of their own watering needs can be a gardener's best friend. Self-watering containers can make watering a breeze.

Plants need moisture at their roots. Self-watering containers are designed to draw roots down to get the moisture for plants to thrive. At the base of these pots there are components to make this possible. An inner shelf, acting as a permeable barrier between the water and the soil, also serves as a way for the plant roots to drain. Allowing the roots to reach for the water (not sit in it) at the bottom of the container prevents root rot.

There are several watering systems that encourage the roots to take up available water. Many garden centers will offer a variety of self-watering containers for sale. They are made of several different types of materials from ceramic to plastic. Choosing the correct size is important. Another important requirement is making certain the reservoir will hold the required amount of water for your choice of plants. Many of these planters come with instructions on how to fill the reservoir. Self-watering pots offer the benefit of being able to add water-soluble nutrients to the reservoir. This is beneficial as it offers consistent nutrients to the plant upon demand.

Often, scheduling time for watering and feeding can prove difficult. A self-watering planter helps with scheduled feeding. Filling the reservoir on a consistent schedule enables the gardener to plan watering more effectively. Some planters have a reservoir on the top or side. When filling a self-watering planter from the top, add water until it flows out or reaches the fill line. If the reservoir lip is on the side, usually inserting a finger or peering into it will alert you about the water level. By checking the reservoir regularly, as well as filling it when necessary, the plant will remain hydrated and healthy.

Create your own self-watering drip container using recyclables. Simply punch holes in the bottom of a milk jug or soda/juice bottle. Fill it with water and nutrients, if necessary. Water your plants well, then set the recycled drip container on the planter soil surface. This will allow the water to slowly drip into the soil as needed, which provides a consistent level of hydration for the plants. Using a planter with a self-watering system or creating your own drip watering device will be a timesaver for the busy gardener.

Railing Hangers and Hooks

Garden spaces can be created on many different levels within the garden. It is a bonus to have raised planting areas in the garden where plants can be observed at eye level—other than always looking (and working) at ground level. One way to make elevated garden spaces is by placing a post in a garden bed or along the perimeter. Putting hooks on the post will allow hanging plants to be used as an extension of the garden—adding depth. There are even decorative posts with baskets attached to the top that encourage homeowners to plant up high. Elevated trailing plants mingling with upright plants in the ground provide exclamation points in the landscape.

Railings are useful when extending the garden as well. Traditionally, wire or wrought iron hay racks or holders were commonly attached to railings, lined with coconut fiber, and planted. These same holders can be utilized in many more creative ways.

In lieu of a liner, try setting pots inside the planters. Each pot can hold a different plant, which increases the charm of the railing planter. Imagine hanging an entire herb garden off your railing—allowing herbs to be within easy reach. Reaching out to pinch a fresh-

grown herb to add to whatever is on the grill—from meats to vegetables—is a gardening pleasure.

Drought-tolerant plantings also do well in railing planters. Mixing plant materials offers texture, color, and form. These drought-tolerant plantings require minimal water and maintenance. If trailing plants are used, pinching them from time to time will keep them compact and healthy. Apply a light mulch to keep excessive water away from succulent leaves.

Assorted hooks placed on a rail or strategically attached to a wall can offer the opportunity to add a pop of unique color or form to new places. Picture a collection of rare plants coming up from a garden bed in elevated hanging pots. Positioning these pots in tiers adds a dimension to an otherwise flat planting. Perhaps insert a small, low-growing evergreen or trailing succulent in the lowest hanging planter. This helps to connect the garden plantings below to the tiered pots above.

The second tier can include a taller, narrow plant or a flowering plant to add fullness. This will draw the eye upwards. This is the perfect level for a pop of color. Using one to three annual plants with long bloom times is quite attractive. If choosing two tiers, a taller, narrow evergreen with space for underplanting adds value. A third tier offers space for whimsical art, natural stones, or even additional plants.

Planters within the garden can tell a story. Including colorful plants that become a focal point allows the creative gardener to explore the possibilities of having seasonal changes for the planted display. Each pot allows space to change out plants throughout the season. Using elevated planters on hooks, non-traditional railing planters, and tiered container plantings makes a statement in the garden.

Hanging Overhead Troughs

Overhead trough gardens are at least as old as the Hanging Gardens of Babylon. These suspended troughs are a great way to gain vertical growing space. They can also be a clever solution for harvesting edible plants and keeping them within arm's reach.

Troughs should be at least 6 inches (15 cm) deep— preferably 8 to 12 inches (20 to 30 cm) deep. They can be made of any lightweight material. Deep metal gutters can be used for this purpose as well as pre-formed plastic window boxes. You can also have wooden troughs custom-built or do-it-yourself.

The troughs can be suspended on chains and hung from a pergola or other structure. They can be mounted in a freestanding system or placed along the edge of a wall or fence line. If you place them along an elevated surface, ensure they will not fall off or tip over by putting some kind of securing bracket or brace in front of them.

Good drainage is a must so be sure there are plenty of drainage holes with whatever type of trough containers you use. Line the trough with a landscape cloth cut to size to hold in the potting mix. In some systems, you can place a tray underneath the trough to collect water and recirculate it.

Watering is a chief concern with these trough containers since they dry out quickly. You may want to install a drip irrigation system to keep them uniformly moist. Use a lightweight potting mix that is designed specifically for container gardening.

Troughs can be chained together so you have several in a row or you may simply place them all at one level. These are normally long and narrow, by definition, so plantings are generally of just one type of plant per trough and planted in a single file.

Trough gardens are useful for growing short edible crops that can be switched out seasonally such as lettuce greens in the cooler months and ever-bearing strawberries in the heat of summer. This is also a good system for growing several different kinds of leafy herbs.

Trough gardens can also be planted with ornamental plants such as annual flowers or, if in a shady spot, you can add in various ferns. You may also like the effect of planting the hanging troughs with vines or trailing groundcovers for a pleasing waterfall effect.

Hypertufa Troughs in the Garden

Hypertufa troughs in the garden can be works of art. Whether they are stand-alone planters or a grouping filled with interesting species of plants, they make a statement. Trough collections have taken on a new prominence as more and more gardeners are using them in the garden.

Today's hypertufa troughs are made from light-weight materials. They can be cast into various shapes from squares to circles, depending on the form you use to create them.

To make your own Hypertufa Trough you will need the following:

- 1½ parts peat moss
- 1½ parts perlite
- 1 part Portland cement
- Concrete reinforcing fibers
- Water
- Dust mask
- Trowel
- Rubber gloves
- Sheeting plastic/drop cloth
- Mold (Styrofoam or an old container)
- Wire brush
- Wheelbarrow or large container for mixing the ingredients

After putting on a dust mask and rubber gloves, put the peat moss, perlite, Portland cement, and a handful of concrete fibers into the wheelbarrow. Mix thoroughly, adding small batches of water to ensure each ingredient is thoroughly moistened, but not overly wet. When this mixture is ready, you should be able to make a ball in your hand that holds together. Squeeze out any excess water. Place the mold on the sheeting plastic upside down. Begin packing the hypertufa mixture onto the outside of the mold (starting at the bottom). Make sure your hypertufa trough is at least 1 to 2 inches (2.5 to 5 cm) thick. Tamp regularly to ensure a consistent thickness on all sides. Flatten the final layer on the top, which will form the bottom, and add a drainage hole.

Pressing a leaf or shell onto the hypertufa trough surface before it has hardened makes an attractive decorative impression. You might also try embedding marbles, sea glass, or mosaic tiles in a unique pattern as a finishing touch.

Cover with a plastic sheet and let it dry for 48 hours in the shade.

Remove the plastic sheeting and then turn the hypertufa planter over to remove the mold. Use a wire brush to soften any sharp edges and wrap again. Place it in a shady area for 2 more days. Unwrap and rinse the planter daily for a minimum of a week to remove any residual lime from the planter. Now your hypertufa planter is ready to use.

Planting in Pots without Drainage

When looking for the perfect pot for the garden, you may find that many do not have a drainage hole. This should not be a deterrent as there are a few options for including these types of pots in your garden.

An attractive container without drainage can be used as a cache pot that is easily refreshed with new plantings seasonally. Many garden centers carry drop-in, pre-planted replacements to accommodate planters of many sizes. These drop-ins offer instant beauty without digging in the soil and are also an alternative for between season or bridge plantings. Popping in a lush, pre-planted container is perfect for a planter without any drainage.

A simple water-filled container adds unexpected value to any garden. Consider using a pot without drainage as a mini water garden. Adding a pond plant or two can add heightened interest to a wide pot that doesn't have any drainage. A simple container with a drop of pond ink and a floating solar fountain is sure to make an elegant addition to any garden. The sound of trickling water in the still of the garden adds a sense of calm. Also, an unexpected water feature will certainly become a favored spot for lingering in the garden.

When strolling in the garden, gather petals, small branches, or even a simple bloom. Artfully tossed onto the water's surface, these garden snippets create a unique, memorable moment. A water-filled planter encourages daily collecting of what is of interest in the garden. Remember to add a mosquito deterrent to the water, as well as to remove the finished garden gleanings regularly. Consider placing colorful planted containers around this water feature to add depth.

There are some plants such, as rice, that can be grown in pots without drainage. Rice grown in a container adds height, volume, and movement—not to mention diversity to any setting. To grow rice, you will need to provide a soil that will hold moisture, such as a good compost or any nutrient-rich soil blend. Fill the planter with the soil—no higher than 2 to 3 inches (5 to 7.5 cm) below the upper edge. Thoroughly add water to the pot. Choose a rice cultivar that is specific to your growing zone. Sow the rice on the surface of the moistened soil. Rice roots need to always be submerged in water—so check the planter often to maintain the right water level. Rice also needs a weed-free environment to grow successfully.

Look for other plants that love damp feet. Keeping plant roots moist is easy in pots that offer no drainage.

Build a Tower Garden

Tower gardens are as creative as the people who build them. The structure and its components can be a typical triangular frame. These frames are usually made of metal with baskets attached for ease of planting. Tower gardens can be planted with annuals that harmonize with each other for an elevated splash of color. Instead of putting these towers away during the winter months, incorporate them in seasonal displays. Adding glass holiday balls, greenery, and berries is a perfect way to add unexpected interest in the winter garden.

Tower gardens do not have to be triangular; they can also form a tower wall. A tower wall garden can be created using a wire grid and recycled plastic bottles. Choose bottles that are uniform in size to determine the size of the tower. Using the wire grid as a foundation, begin preparing the bottles. Leave the cap on the first bottle. Cut the bottom off the first bottle and pierce the side so water drains easily. Turn the bottle so that the cap is down. Add potting soil and leave room for the second bottle. Pierce the cap of the second recycled bottle and remove the bottom. Add potting soil and stack this bottle in the potting soil of the first bottle. Continue layering the bottles to the desired height. Secure the bottles sporadically with wire to the metal fencing or grid.

Once the bottles are secured to the grid, the uppermost bottle should have the bottom cut off as well as a hole pierced in the cap. This bottle should not have potting soil added as it is the point for adding your water and nutrients. Cut a slit or circle in the sides of the lower bottles and insert the root balls of your small plants leaving the foliage to hang out. This tower will keep your vertical series of plants well-watered and fed using minimal space.

Another option is a cinder (cement) block tower. Stacking cinder blocks into specific shapes with sporadic openings throughout offers a truly creative tower planting. Stagger the cinder blocks and occasionally leave the short side jutting out as a space for planting. Use a weed-blocking material, chicken wire with coir, or felt to line these pockets and plant away. Children of all ages and heights can enjoy a tower garden such as this. Planting can become a family affair. It is wonderful to see children planting and adding plants throughout the season. If the planting pockets are accessible, it can quickly become a bonding experience. This can easily become a work of art that is ever-changing.

Create a garden tower by layering stone, bricks, or pavers into a spiral cylinder. Add potting soil to create a multi-layered surface for planting herbs, assorted vegetables, or even a work of floral art during the garden season. This semi-permanent structure can be utilized to grow a collection of dwarf plants like a micro tomato, specialty basil, herbs for tea, gourmet lettuce, or miniature ornamental plants. This is perfect for a specialty garden which showcases rare or specimen plants.

A tower garden can be in any shape imaginable. A wall tower, a physical tower, or even a spiral tower—these are just a few options that tap into the creativity of the homeowner.

Planters on Wheels

A portable garden comes in handy for many reasons. One advantage of moving some winter annual plantings to a cooler spot is to extend their season when the weather heats up. As tree canopies begin to fill out in the spring, moving these plants to a more shaded location offers a buffer from the strong sun. The dappled light is often just enough to keep these cool-season plants happy and growing longer.

The summer sun can be quite strong. There are many options of plants that are bred for full sun applications. As our climate shifts, some plants that would normally require full sun might appreciate a buffer from at least the strongest afternoon sun. In warmer climates, plants such as geraniums appreciate and do quite well in semi-shade. As the season progresses and tree canopies increase, plants that would tolerate semi-shade, might appreciate more sun. The ability to move a planter on wheels makes it easy to satisfy the changing light needs of a plant.

Creating a planter on wheels is simple. Most garden centers sell plant saucers with casters. Make certain these ready-made saucers will allow water to drain away from the plant roots. There are also pots with wheels already built-in that are readily available online or at your favorite garden center. These often have a reservoir at the base for watering.

Consider using eclectic recycled items such as an old wheelbarrow for cool-season vegetables. The wheels make it easier to shift these planters to areas of the garden where they would benefit from a little shade in warmer months and more sun in cooler months.

Consider using plastic crates or even recycled wooden boxes. Adding wheels to the undersides of these is easy. Make certain the casters or wheels can accommodate the weight of the plant and soil (when it is fully saturated). You will need a marker, a drill, the appropriate size drill bit, heavyweight casters or wheels, and enough landscape fabric to line the container. Mark the placement of the holes, drill through, and attach the wheels. Line the container with landscape fabric to hold the soil in place and plant your new planter on wheels. Doing it yourself allows the homeowner to add a little whimsy by using unusual items not normally found in the garden.

Consider adding wheels to a large pot. Drill holes into the bottom of a container of your choice, add a washer, casters, and then the soil. The value of having large pots on wheels is greatly appreciated when growing tropical plants. Having a pot on wheels makes it easy to move weather-sensitive plants inside at the end of the growing season.

Utilizing planters on wheels allows any small-space garden to change by merely rolling a planter to a different location in the garden.

Fabric Containers and Bags

Many alternatives to traditional pots are readily available. These options include recycled fiber pots, reclaimed plastic, and various other recycled materials. There are many benefits to using recycled fabric containers and bags.

Fabric pots offer optimal drainage thereby decreasing the risk of root rot. A few other benefits include encouraging healthy bacteria to thrive in the soil and maintaining a cool environment for healthy roots to grow.

The budget-wise gardener might consider using reusable shopping bags. Most grocery stores offer these affordable alternatives. These bags are often made from recycled plastic such as soda bottles. A few holes placed in the bottom and sides of the bag will allow water to drain away freely. These bags can be placed inside of a decorative cache pot and will usually last a season or two. Easily dispose of the soil inside the container by emptying the bag into the garden at the end of the season. This disposable resource can then be recycled again—perhaps as another bag.

Another type of fabric planter bag is made of recycled fibers. These grow bags offer portability as they are lightweight, colorful, and now made in various sizes. These pots are porous which allows the roots to have good air circulation. The air that flows through these containers encourages natural root pruning as the plants grow. Root pruning helps plants grow healthy, sturdy roots.

There are plastic and fabric bags that can be mounted on a wall or fence. Consider hanging a trio or grouping together. Usually, these wall pockets are made of recyclable materials. The back is normally lined to maintain moisture at the root zone.

Some of the latest versions of these fabric containers offer side pockets as well. In a fabric pot with a side pocket, consider growing a companion plant. A tomato plant with a dwarf basil can certainly be a space-saving combination. A planting like this allows for fewer pots in a smaller space. Consider keeping an old or worn fabric pot in the garden to place plant debris that will be composted. The value of a fabric container continues even at the end of its planter life.

When the growing season ends, fabric containers can easily be emptied for storage as well. Dump the soil into the garden or compost pile. If the pots are wet, place them in the sun to dry. Using a brush, dislodge any loose soil and flatten them. Then store them in a dry space for the next season. Unlike traditional pots, a flattened stack of fabric containers takes up minimal storage space. Fabric containers allow for extra flexibility in the garden or even in a garden bed.

Fabric bags and containers are quite useful and can be used for different purposes in the garden. There are even fabric containers made of reinforced weed-blocking fabric that are sturdy enough for growing larger shrubs and small trees. These make it easy for growers and gardeners to minimize root damage when transporting or transplanting them.

Lighten Up Large Containers with Fillers

Large plant pots are the easiest to care for and promote healthier plants. They have more root space to grown in. A few generously sized planters are less maintenance and less work than several small pots. Large pots also dry out less quickly and look more abundant and less hodge-podge. (See Coordinating a Pot Palette on page 176.)

However, large planters can be quite heavy. If you are gardening on a deck, balcony, or rooftop, then the weight of a container, its soil, and the water to fully saturate the soil can be quite significant. Even when at ground level, large pots filled with wet soil can be cumbersome and hard to move or work around.

To address this, consider not filling the entire interior of a planter with soil. Instead, look at placing various fillers in it to take up the bottom third or so. Take note though that you want the container to still be free-draining.

In the past, it was common gardening advice to put rocks or broken pottery shards in the bottom of containers. That practice has since been shown to cause water to be trapped inside the pot and cause root rot.

Your containers should have several drainage holes. If your pot only has one or a few holes, you can add more by using a drill. (Use a diamond drill bit for ceramics or clay pots.) To hold in the soil so it doesn't leak out of the drainage holes, you can cut a circle of landscape fabric, weed cloth, coffee filter, fine-mesh screening, or other permeable material, and place that over the holes.

There are planter inserts that you can purchase at garden centers to set down inside the pot to lift the overall soil level. You can also create one yourself, if you are handy.

Other materials that can be placed in the bottom of large containers to take up space, lighten the planter, and create an air pocket below the soil line include emptied and crushed aluminum cans, plastic milk jugs, plastic water or soda bottles, and a stack of nursery pots turned upside down.

Blocks of foam can also be used as filler, but do not use loose Styrofoam pellets. This is for the same reasons given above for not using rocks or pottery shards, but also because if the pot tips over in a storm the pellets will escape and pollute the environment. They will also mix with the bottom layer of soil and can be very difficult to separate later. You can use these pellets if they are placed inside a plastic bag and then inside another bag and tied tightly shut to eliminate any possibility that they might escape.

"Lighten up" is a good principle for the way we live our lives and can make your container gardening easier as well.

CHAPTER 2

Creative Flower Growing

BEAUTY IS AN essential element for green space in the city, though it is one aspect of urban gardening that is often downplayed or only included as an afterthought—so much so that, to many people, even the term "urban garden" conjures up images of vegetable plots and mini-farms. The concept that ornamental gardening is somehow less worthy than food gardening is false.

The healing properties of time spent in gorgeous gardens are as valuable today as they were at any other time in human history. In the following pages, we not only tell you how to grow beautiful gardens, we also aim to give you permission to grow flowers simply for flowers' sake. Continue on with your journey to find ways to fit flower gardening into even the smallest of spaces.

No-Fuss Perennial Plantings

A self-sufficient garden that returns every year is a gardener's dream. Using easy-care perennials can make a no-fuss garden a reality. The dependability of the no-fuss perennial garden has many benefits and virtues.

A perennial garden saves money. Depending on your taste, it can be filled with various types of perennials that bloom throughout the season. There are many clumping plants that will increase in size over time. Clumping perennials can be divided and transplanted throughout the garden each spring. This is a great way to have certain plants repeated in various spots throughout your plantings. Consider sporadically placing your favorite perennials throughout the garden to add interest through repetition.

Perennials that spread by rhizomes are also great for no-fuss plantings. Monarda, for example, spreads by underground roots, which quickly cover anywhere it is allowed to roam. It is easy to stop it from spreading where you don't want it to go. The rhizomes are generally right under the surface of the soil and are not difficult to dig out. Make certain you remove all of the root sections, or it will quickly return. Alternatively, these spreading perennial plants can be used to minimize weed growth or inexpensively cover a problem area.

Self-sowing perennials add value to any garden bed as well. For example, Rudbeckias and Echinacea cultivars are perennials that provide abundant color in the garden. Allowing the seed heads to develop and remain on these plants will provide food during the fall and winter months for migrating birds. By leaving seed heads to be eaten by wildlife or dispersed naturally by winter weather, lets Mother Nature do the garden design. This creates a unique no-fuss perennial garden providing a color palette that changes every year.

A no-fuss perennial garden encourages the gardener to choose plants wisely. Selecting perennials that are drought-tolerant and offer multi-season interest enables the gardener to spend more time enjoying the garden. Drought-tolerant perennials generally rely on minimal rainfall, only requiring water in temperature extremes. These plants are often used in out-of-the-way places where watering can be difficult. There is no need to sacrifice beauty when using hardy perennials that thrive in less-than-perfect conditions. Some plants to consider include ornamental grasses, liatris, and tall sedum cultivars.

Consider perennials that add colorful blooms and changing foliage colors for multi-season interest. Starting in autumn, think about what plants might offer winter interest. Bark, seed heads, or even dried foliage can go a long way when nothing else is in bloom.

Using perennials that have evergreen leaves adds a lot of winter interest. Some of these plants like the hellebore cultivars will bloom in late winter. Perennial bulbs with differing bloom times should be added to the no-fuss border. Look for appropriate bulbs that naturalize in your hardiness zone. Perennial bulbs will usher in displays of blooms to weave the seasons together. Choosing the right fuss-free perennials is important for a garden that provides effortless beauty.

Window Box Recipe

Window boxes are great for bringing out the creative spirit in the gardener. There are basic combinations that are conservative in structure. However, there are also more flamboyant window boxes that seem to really pop and come to life. Unique combinations should contain a few basic components. The perfect recipe for a window box begins with height, density, and abundance. Sometimes this is considered the thriller, the filler, and of course, the spiller.

It is important to think about the size of the window box. Plant roots need to be accommodated for optimum health and growth. If the window box is narrow, consider plants with high-impact bloom, but minimal roots. Some sort of spiller will add a little interest to draw the eye beneath the bloom. A robust foliage plant or vine that skirts the blooms above is a great choice. A smaller, more refined window box is perfect for a simple planting.

Abundant, statement window boxes require more plants that play well with others. The larger the window box, the more plant options will increase. Placement of your plant choices make a big difference and will vary according to the lighting conditions. The fun begins with the thriller. Using something like an ornamental grass, a plant with spikey blooms, or even garden art are great ideas. Consider the structure of the thriller.

Know what the ultimate height will be—including the bloom. If you are using a spikey plant, make sure that it does not obscure the window or railing beyond, unless this is intentional. If you want to block a window for privacy, choosing the proper plant is important. Airy or feathery foliage allows coverage without totally blocking a view. Blooms on spires create movement in the wind and draw the eye upwards.

Adding plants with girth and spread, the fillers, can add untold interest to the window box. Common options include interesting foliage plants (without significant flowers) that increasingly fill out over the length of the growing season. Add to this a complementary mid-height plant with stunning blooms. If the blooms are small but prolific, a mid-planter color sweep can create a stunning effect. A plant with a short spike or wide bloom with textured foliage can add depth and make the middle section of the window box look three-dimensional.

The middle of the planter also allows room for trying plants that welcome a bit of shade, provided by the filler plants. Partial shading can also be provided by neighboring plant foliage. Some plants that would normally require some shade, can thrive here with a bit of a semi-shade buffer. Keep in mind, these plants all need to be watered and fed regularly for optimal performance. Good maintenance will encourage the plants to remain stunning all season long.

The spiller could also be the garnish for any window box recipe. There is always the option of playing it safe and using a basic green, non-blooming trailing plant. The leaf shape could be exciting on its own. No need to be boring now when there are choices. Try playing off or highlighting one of the colors included in the existing composition. With new trailing cultivars available today there are many options such as silver foliage, variegated foliage, and even textured trailing foliage. As with any recipe, adjusting the ingredients to taste makes it your own.

Self-Sowing Annuals

Need long-blooming color in the garden? Annual flowers are often desired in the garden for almost season-long color. As the weather around the world continues to shift, some annuals are beginning to be hardier and will survive in even more regions. Within weeks after planting, annuals will quickly grow and fill space in the garden with blooms. Usually, these plants are easy care and perform extremely well. When annuals finish blooming some will drop their seed. This is called self-sowing.

These annual seedlings nestle into place whenever they fall. Setting roots, they begin to grow prolifically. One thing to remember, annuals do not reliably return. Annual plants are bred to grow quickly for a season. Any seeds that sprout can be easily dug up and transplanted. These seedlings can be used as filler plants wherever they are needed.

Self-sown seedlings, like those of nigella, bachelor's buttons, larkspur, poppies, and others, can soften the edge of a path and provide unexpected bloom in some unexpected places. These blooms will complement most plantings. There are other self-sowing annuals such as cleome and cosmos that will serve as support staff within the sunny border. There are even some cool-season annuals that have been known to self-sow and return unexpectedly, such as violas and pansy cultivars.

Incorporating self-sowing annuals into the garden can create a meadow within the border. Planting specific spots in the garden with annual plants that are known to set seed adds value to the garden. Applying a good fertilizer will help keep these plants healthy. At the end of the season, consider crushing the dried flower heads and sprinkle the seeds on the surface of the garden bed where you have bare spots. Also, consider leaving the annual in place to drop its seed randomly during the dormant months.

Seedlings of self-sowing plants will often not be true to the original cultivar. Sometimes a seedling will differ in bloom color or growth habit. The resulting seedlings might be taller, shorter, or even have a bicolor bloom.

Self-sowing annuals are also quite easy to notice if they are unwanted in a specific area of the garden. Pay attention to the leaf of the annual during the season. When identifying a seedling, the leaf is a great way to know if a tiny plant is a desired seedling or a weed. Need a gift for a fellow gardener? Consider potting up a few of the excess seedlings and sharing them with others.

Depending on the climate, some of the annuals you might consider adding, for a diverse palette of striking flowers, are poppies, bachelor's buttons (*Centaurea cyanus*), larkspur, or flax. Perhaps they will self-sow in your garden.

Long-Blooming Shrubs

Shrubs often take up considerable space in the urban landscape. Some homeowners want long-lasting interest that pops in their garden. This can be through plant structure, color, or bloom. Shrubs that offer long-season blooms add value to the landscape.

Some shrubs are deciduous and provide interesting bark color in the garden before the leaves emerge. Other shrubs are evergreen with textural interest. While not exactly a bloom, this foliage adds season-long color. Many shrubs have foliage that will set the stage for the blooms to come. When the flowers bloom, the leaves become a backdrop. There are some shrubs that will produce a second flush of blooms, if the first set of flowers are sheared immediately after they finish. Other shrubs require virtually no maintenance, but bloom sporadically throughout the season.

The late fall or winter landscape can often be seen with shades of pink, red, or white blooms on foundation shrubs. Spring is welcomed with flowering shrubs in many different colors including shades of purple, orange, and yellow. These blooms are the perfect way to add a touch of color as the rest of the garden awakens.

Some shrubs produce a prolific amount of tubular and quite showy blooms. These shrubs attract specific birds and pollinators—adding to their impact in the border. The colorful blooms are even more noticeable when birds dip inside the narrow blooms to partake of their nectar. On some cultivars, the blooms can change color before falling off like confetti to the garden floor.

The larger blooms of some shrubs will punctuate the landscape with noticeable color. Sometimes starting early in the season, large blooms will pop with color and make an empty shrub border come to life. To have the best blooms, certain shrub cultivars require pruning to remove the seed heads from the previous season.

Large-leaved shrubs with noticeably larger-than-life blooms are a winning combination in the landscape. It is a sight to behold when variegated foliage shrubs bloom. The landscape becomes punctuated with color and sometimes can even be accompanied by scent.

Long-blooming shrubs are adaptable to many different light conditions. Many require 6 to 8 hours of sun. There are even some which require part shade. When planting, consider what shrubs will complement in the garden upon their maturity. A large, long-blooming shrub can become a focal point amid an evergreen garden. Using such a shrub can minimize the need for smaller plantings. Try using a long-blooming shrub when considering low-maintenance gardening. Usually, these shrubs require minimal care, if the conditions are right.

Using shrub blooms as fresh-cut flowers is a way of bringing a spot of color indoors. There are even shrubs with blooms that are great for drying and can be used in floral arrangements later. These long-blooming shrubs bring considerable value to any landscape.

Drought-Tolerant Landscape

Many homeowners want to have a landscape that always looks good. The requirements usually include minimal upkeep and that the landscape is great for entertaining. A drought-tolerant landscape fits the bill and is a style that has become quite popular. Each climate region will offer various options for soil amendments, plant material, and mulch so gardeners can create a drought-tolerant landscape.

Drought tolerant does not mean having totally arid conditions. This term means that plants can survive with minimal water usage. In areas where the climate conditions are moist and rainfall is ample, plant selection can be quite diverse. Plants will have no difficulty performing without additional water. Providing a mulch of some type will keep the roots of these plants hydrated. From trees to shrubs, drought-tolerant plantings can be lush with plenty of greenery and blooming plants.

In areas where rainfall is moderate, a different type of drought tolerance can be observed. While some of the plant material is similar, there are more options. In this climate, succulents are offered in various forms. Succulent groundcovers in these areas easily spread and cover the soil surface. Mulching in these areas can be quite beneficial. When moisture is retained, usually minimal plant maintenance is required. Plants grown in these conditions will bloom and rarely need deadheading. The only maintenance that might be required is trimming to maintain shape or form. Some drought-tolerant plants can maintain lush foliage for at least three seasons of the year. This plant material can add beauty especially during the winter months. The diversity found in the foliage, whether it is the color or texture, can be the perfect backdrop for enjoying the garden in any season.

Many people consider extremely hot, arid areas perfect for drought-tolerant plantings. There are specific plants to use for a drought-tolerant landscape that would survive under these conditions. The leaves, stems, and roots hold onto water,

saving it for a much-needed drink later, when it is necessary for healthy growth. In conditions like this, planting in lean soil provides the required growing environment for plants to thrive. Some of these plants are long blooming and thrive on minimal care.

Ornamental grasses should be considered when deciding on materials for drought-tolerant plantings. Using a diverse collection of grasses is a guarantee that the garden will have interest throughout. Try using different heights, leaf blade colors, as well as textures to achieve excitement in the garden. There are some grasses that have slender seed heads that move in the breeze. Other cultivars offer plump, brush-type heads that will add architectural interest to the garden. Some ornamental grasses produce seed heads that add seasonal interest. Removing the seed heads later in the season will help keep these grasses from self-sowing.

Mulching options are different depending on the region. Many drought-tolerant gardens use minimal amounts of wood mulch. Instead, pebbles, river rock, and sometimes even sand are commonly used for drought-tolerant plantings. Each of these materials enable the soil to drain quickly, allowing the upper surface to remain a bit dry. In an urban setting, using various forms of rock as a form of mulch has its virtues—such as easier weed removal. However, removing fallen leaves from nearby trees will require careful raking or blowing to clear out the rock mulch.

A drought-tolerant planting should be carefully thought out when in the planning stages.

Fragrance Freeways

Fragrance in the garden comes in many forms. Trees, vines, shrubs, and even smaller plantings that have scent provide added value to any garden. A lingering scent will encourage anyone in the garden to consider it a place to stay and enjoy. Whether you choose to have a single fragrant feature or a border of fragrance, there are a few factors to consider. The best location, which path is most traveled, and ease of maintenance are just a few items to consider when plotting the placement of fragrant features in the garden.

Location is important to the enjoyment of any scented plant. Imagine the scent of a single potted plant on a nearby table. Planting only one gives the nose a slight tickle. Adding three plants in a larger pot really wafts the scent to the nose and fills the area. This allows the fragrance to be enjoyed without being up close. Plants with scent that are placed in pots can be arranged in groupings for maximum effect or scattered throughout the space. The more powerful the scent, the fewer plants required. Having fragrance in an enclosed space often sets the mood. And in an enclosed space, the scent of even the smallest plant can be intensified.

For more intense fragrances consider a mass planting positioned where the wind can move the fragrance throughout the garden—even with the lightest breeze. There is no mistaking the power of scent when plants are installed in swaths. A large planting of a fragrant plant magnifies the scent. When gardening with fragrant plants consider their bloom time. This will allow the fragrances to shine and not overlap. Each fragrance should have an individual identity and not compete with another.

Placing scented plants along well-traveled pathways can draw people into the garden. Soothing the mind or evoking a pleasant thought, scented plants tap into our senses. Fragrant flowers are perfect for cutting, it's easy to create simple bouquets to bring indoors and enjoy.

If creating bouquets is not to your liking, you can still enjoy fragrance from the garden. Another creative way is to place the scented plant near a window. Imagine simply opening a window and inviting fragrance in. This is one of the most practical ways to enjoy the added value of a scented plant in the garden. The key is keeping fragrant shrubs at a height where the fragrance can be accessible. Sometimes this will require pruning after they bloom, so the plant can prepare for the next season's floral show.

In addition to perennials and shrubs, there are a few trees that provide fragrance via their blooms or even from their foliage. Fragrant blooms can be insignificant, barely noticeable, yet exuding a sweet scent. On smaller plants, pruning after they bloom is easy and can sometimes encourage continuous bloom. On larger specimen trees or shrubs, garden hygiene is important. Remove fallen remnants of the finished blooms to avoid the spread of disease and pests.

Cool-Season Annuals

Annuals are not just for summer gardens. Depending on your climate and hardiness zone, cooler temperatures are a welcome relief to many plants. Cool-season annuals thrive on the moderate temperatures that occur in the spring as well as in autumn. These milder temperatures are required for certain plants to set buds for upcoming seasonal beauty. Most of these plants are frost tolerant. When the temperatures drop to freezing, cool-season annuals will pause and not grow above ground until the temperatures moderate. Once the temperatures rise, new buds will set, and the plants will begin blooming again.

If growing from seed, cool-season annuals are usually sown in the late summer. This allows the seeds to germinate, seedlings to grow, and plants to survive and thrive in the cooler temperatures ahead.

If you are looking for low- to medium-height, cool-season annuals, consider the colorful pansy, (*Viola ×wittrockiana*). These plants, or Johnny jump ups (*Viola tricolor*), are easy to sow and they will often reseed in the garden. In addition to cool temperatures, these plants need 100 days to grow before they will bloom. Seed gently tossed in a pot or in a prepared site in late summer will have violas blooming about three months later and then the plants will set seed—starting more plants growing in late winter (in milder gardens). Other options of low growing, cool-season annuals to consider are:

- Forget-Me-Nots (*Myosotis sylvatica*)
- Stock (*Matthiola incana*)
- Love-in-a-Mist (*Nigella damascena*)

Mid-height, cool-season plants are terrific backdrops for the lower plants. Calendula or pot marigolds are all-time favorites to start early and enjoy throughout the season. Growing 10 inches (25 cm) or more, these flowers make a great bouquet and are beautiful in fresh salads. If a mild winter is anticipated, calendula seeds can be sown in autumn. Consider growing dwarf sweet peas (*Lathyrus odoratus*) in pots for a fragrant, cool-season option. This is a great alternative to providing a trellis or stake for the taller sweet peas to grow up. A few other options for mid-height, cool-season plants are:

- African Daisy (*Osteospermum* sp.)
- Dusty Miller (*Jacobaea maritima* syn. *Senecio cineraria*)
- Flowering Kale (*Brassica oleracea* Acephala group)

Taller cool-season annuals take a bit longer to grow, however they are worth the wait. These are sown in the fall or when the ground has thawed in early spring. These annuals will sometimes need staking, but often they simply lean into neighboring plants. Snapdragons (*Antirrhinum majus*) stand tall and have amazing flower colors. From soft pinks to bicolored yellow and white, snapdragons are a great cut flower and are used in early spring bouquets. Perhaps consider using an assortment of tall, cool-season annuals such as:

- Larkspur (*Consolida ajacis*)
- Sweet Annie (*Artemisia annua*)
- Corn Poppy (*Papaver rhoeas*)

It is important to decide what cultivar, height, and bloom time of cool-season annuals to grow in the early spring (or sometimes late autumn) garden. Scattering seeds will create a unique display that welcomes a new season and can be rewarding. The beauty of a springtime floral display is a cheery sight in a vase or as a larger arrangement, especially when all the flowers have been grown in your garden.

Color in the Winter Garden

The urban garden can be an eclectic palette for color. In the winter, color livens up the barren garden, whether it's from berries, bark, or garden ornaments. No matter the size of your space, finding ways to add winter color can be fun and beneficial to wildlife, too. Trees and shrubs add color through the fruits they bear, their leaves, or even their blooms. Some small trees for urban landscapes have brightly colored stems that can be quite vivid, especially against a backdrop of snow. Choose a statement tree that looks good tucked into a corner or holding center stage.

Shrubs known for their showy colored berries when little is in bloom are another way to add color to the winter garden. Lingering throughout the winter, birds are attracted to these shrubs as a food source. Slow-growing choices that top out at 5 to 10 feet (1.5 to 3 m) tall are good options for small urban landscapes.

Shrubs with striking red or yellow stems during the colder months can also provide food and shelter for wildlife. These shrubs also deliver quite the statement in the winter garden. Golden-twig dogwood, *Cornus sericea* 'Flaviramea' has yellow stems that are stunning in the urban garden. They are one of many favorites in the winter garden.

Evergreens, whether needled or broadleaved, are delightful in the midst of the winter season. Positioning is everything, especially for broadleaved shrubs such as rhododendrons, camellias, azaleas, boxwoods, and others. They need to be protected from strong winds to prevent desiccation and leaf curl. For small urban gardens, choose shrubs with winter interest that grow from 5 to 12 feet (1.5 to 3.7 m) if left unpruned.

Perennials that begin blooming sometime during the winter or early spring, or those with semi-evergreen or evergreen foliage, are a wonderful way to add color to the winter garden. Personal favorites like hellebores, epimediums, ajugas, and sedums come to mind.

Groundcovers create a colorful underplanting for winter-blooming shrubs, beneath larger trees, or along walkways. Their foliage often graces the ground in various shades of green. There are also many evergreen groundcovers to choose from, no matter which region of the globe you call home. Shearing the foliage from time to time in the early spring will generate lots of new growth that will look extra lush and green when winter arrives.

There are several bulb plants that can brighten the winter landscape as well, including snow drops, *Galanthus nivalis*, which are one of the first heralds of spring in cold climates, crocus, and netted iris, *Iris reticulata*, all of which are early to rise and provide color in the late winter garden.

Winter Sowing

Sowing seeds in the middle of winter is a great distraction from the weather outdoors. There are two ways to sow seeds in winter. The traditional way of sowing seeds during the winter months is with a soilless mix, seed trays, grow lights, and seeds. Setting up an area to accommodate 3 to 4 months of succession-sown seeds for the garden can be exciting. Counting down the months backwards from the last freeze and frost dates is also important.

There is an alternate way to sow seeds during winter. Sow them outdoors. Outdoor winter seed sowing is quite simple. A recycled milk jug, a soilless mix, duct tape, a nail, permanent markers, a small piece of clear plastic, and seeds are all that is required. Usually, this type of winter sowing is done in late January and February, depending on your climate and hardiness zone. There is a second period for sowing outdoor seeds which is in late March and April.

Use a clear jug or bottle for winter sowing. Transparent recyclables such as liter soda bottles and juice jugs will work just fine. If the container is opaque, light will be unavailable to the seedlings. Slice the container in the middle from left to right, leaving a 1- or 2-inch (2.5- or 5-cm) hinge. When using a milk jug, cutting the container and leaving the hinge just below the handle helps when transporting the containers outdoors.

To provide ample drainage, puncture holes in the bottom of the jug or container with the nail or other sharp instrument. Add 3 to 4 inches (7.5 to 10 cm) of soilless mix inside the container. It is important to use a soilless mix to achieve the best results within the container. It is not recommended to use potting soil, moisture-enhanced soil blends, or soil enhanced with fertilizer. Allow room for the seedlings to grow. Keep in mind that once germination occurs, the seedlings will sprout and need headroom. These seedlings will stay in the container until it is time to plant them outside. Generously moisten the soilless mix with warm water and gently tamp down. If the growing mix settles to less than 3 to 4 inches (7.5 to 10 cm), add more until it reaches the desired level.

Scatter the seeds on top of the soil. It is important to make certain there is seed to soilless mix contact. If the seeds are large, add a light layer of moistened soilless mix on top. Using the permanent marker, identify on the container which seeds are inside. Take the duct tape and seal the cut sides tightly. Using the small piece of clear plastic, cover the top of the jug and wrap it with duct tape. Gently poke a few holes in the top for air circulation. Immerse the jugs in a basin of water overnight to ensure the soilless mix is thoroughly moistened.

Move the jugs outside to a protected area such as the deck, in an open cold frame, near a compost pile, or even in the flower bed. The freezing and thawing cycle of an average winter will encourage the seeds to spout and grow. The sun should create condensation inside of the jugs. If there is no condensation, add a few more slits for air to circulate within the container.

Once the seedlings begin to grow, add more slits to the clear jugs to encourage hardening off. Winter seed sowing can take place outside, just as nature intended.

Direct-Sowing

Sowing the seeds for plants that you love is a fun activity to do with family and friends. It is simple, cost-effective and, if done at the right time, it can be quite a success. The hardest part might be deciding on the colors, size, and type of seeds that you will direct-sow.

The first step to sowing seeds is site selection. If the selected seed requires 6 or more hours of sun, then a full-sun location should be chosen. Part-shade plants can be sown at the feet of taller plants to take advantage of all available space in the garden. If a seed requires shade, try placing it in a partly shaded site. Some plants have proven to be quite flexible in their light needs.

Soil preparation is one of the keys to successfully sowing seeds. Prepare the soil by incorporating compost, manure, humus, or a soil conditioner. If the soil is mostly clay, adding these amendments is important for breaking up the clay and allowing the young roots to settle in. Obtain a soil test if you are considering creating a bed from scratch. A soil test will outline what the percentage of the soil components are, how acidic or alkaline (the pH) the soil is, as well as what nutrients are needed. Knowing the pH of the soil is important. The pH range that most plants find optimal is slightly acidic (between 6.0 and 7.0).

Seed selection is the third and most crucial step. Identify what seeds you want to sow and read the seed packet carefully. Not all seeds need to be covered with soil. Some seeds require light to germinate. Also, the size of the seeds will determine how deeply they will need to be planted. If seeds are planted too deep, they will not germinate. There are even some seeds that need to be scarified, softened, or nicked to help them germinate. Softening a seed coating can be as simple as soaking it overnight in a bowl of water. Some seeds that should be nicked, scratched, or scarified are sweet peas, nasturtiums, lupines, moon vine, and morning glories. Reading the seed packet will provide specific instructions on which seed preparation method is required.

Sow at the correct depth and spacing that as listed on the seed packet. Spacing is important for the seedling roots. If the roots are too crowded and not given the space to grow, the plant will be stunted or not perform as expected.

Keep the newly seeded area moist for rapid germination. Once the seedlings have emerged, water them with a gentle mist. This is just the beginning of your direct-seeded garden. This is the perfect activity for a group or a family—to encourage watching nature evolve from a seed.

CHAPTER 3

Food Growing

L ET'S FACE IT, food growing in the city is a steep challenge for many gardeners. It can be discouraging to deal with the pressure from pests, the threat of theft, and the harsh growing environment, but, oh, the rewards! Is there anything better tasting than a fresh tomato, sun-ripened, and plucked from your own garden?

We know it is not always easy, yet we think it is worth the effort and hope you will take on at least one of the suggested edible gardening projects that follow. This section also outlines several ways to answer the common problems that urban food growers might encounter— from composting safely to growing carrots with no suitable ground space. Dig in and grow on.

Salad Tables

Salad tables put a buffet of edible greens within reach right at waist height. Think of them as a raised bed that allows easy access and convenience for growing and harvesting lettuce, radishes, and much more. Raising the growing area off the ground is ideal for those with mobility issues and for those who have a problem with rabbits and other vermin chewing on their tender greens. If you are growing plants on a balcony, salad tables are great for raising your edible plants up to the railing height so they can receive full sun exposure as well.

Salad tables can also help you extend your growing season. Most lettuces prefer the cooler, shoulder seasons of spring and fall and then will bolt (set flower and go to seed) in the heat of the summer. Only mild climates will see lettuce grow through the winter. In colder areas it will die back or at least go dormant. A salad table can be moved around the urban garden to be in more shade or more sun as needed to adjust for seasonal variations.

Depending on how deep or shallow you make your salad table, it can be used to also grow other edible plants such as radishes, scallions, and herbaceous cutting herbs like basil, cilantro, or parsley. You can also use it to grow some fairly shallow-rooted ornamental annuals such as marigolds, larkspur, and celosia.

You can purchase a salad table kit or put your own together with a few basic carpentry skills. It is basically a wooden frame or bottomless box on legs. The box (or frame) should be no wider than 3 feet (1 m) across, but it can be as long as you like. The frame should be at least 4 to 6 inches (10 to 15 cm) in depth. The salad table frame should be lined on the bottom with landscape fabric and mesh, window screening, or wire hardware cloth to retain the potting mix and still allow for good drainage.

The height of the salad table is up to you—whatever height you feel is most comfortable. If you are gardening with children, you might even create a shorter salad table that is easier for them to access. You can even set the wooden frame on sawhorses or attach it to sturdy legs.

You can also construct a smaller salad box that can sit on a side table or bench. Just ensure that there is adequate drainage and that it will not damage the table surface below it. As a precaution, you could sit the salad box on a few bricks or pot feet to raise it up to help with drainage.

Whether you are using a salad box or table, growing and harvesting greens is a terrific way to grow in a small space. Enjoy your raised bed on legs by snipping some fresh spinach for a salad or a few arugula leaves to use as a pizza topping. *Bon appétit!*

Root Vegetables in Containers

Containers can be the urban gardener's best friend—especially when it comes to growing edible plants. The possibilities for container gardening have increased, particularly when you consider growing root vegetables. Here are a few good reasons for growing root vegetables in a container. Since many new gardeners are unsure about growing directly in the soil, growing vegetables in a container allows you to use the best soil for your desired root crop. If pest issues develop, they are more noticeable, as well as easier to control.

Of course, growing root vegetables in a container includes the opportunity to grow many varieties of potatoes. Potatoes come in different colors, sizes, and are grown for many purposes. To start, cut up your seed potato so that each piece has one eye that is starting to grow. Expose each seed potato piece to the air for an hour or so to allow it to develop a callous. Add about 4 to 6 inches (10 to 15 cm) of soil to the bottom of the container. Then lay the potato piece on the surface of the soil with the eye facing up. Add a minimum of 3 inches (7.5 cm) of soil covering the entire piece of the seed potato. In a few days, foliage will begin to grow. Continue adding soil to the container covering the potato until the container is full.

When the foliage begins to yellow, the potatoes are ready to be harvested. Some fabric containers have a side window that allows you to see the potatoes grow. Cover this window after taking a peek so the potatoes don't turn green. This is a terrific project to grow with children.

Why stop at potatoes? Growing radishes or carrots in a container are easier than you think. Some of the newer carrot cultivars come in exciting colors and are shorter in length. Carrots will need a container that is a minimum of 6 inches (15 cm) deep. Sow the seeds on top of the soil, then add a small amount of lightweight compost to protect the seeds from hungry birds. Once they begin to grow, pull out or thin the carrots to allow space for them to mature. Radishes grow quickly and are one of the earliest vegetables to grow. Both are great vegetables to grow with children or even new gardeners.

Beets are another great choice for growing in a container. The above ground foliage is edible as well as the underground beet. There are so many colors and cultivars of beets, and their ease of growth makes them a must-have for the container garden. Radishes, carrots, and beets are best sown during the cooler months of the growing season, like spring and fall.

Did you know that you can grow garlic in a container? Plant garlic in a 6- to 8-inch (15- to 20-cm) deep container. They should be started during the cooler temperatures. Garlic, as well as onions, can be planted closely together in a container. Use the green flower stalks (called scapes) for cooking or even in salads. Garlic and onions require 6 hours of sun to thrive in the garden.

Turnips are another root vegetable that is easily grown in a container. You can also harvest the greens once they have been touched by frost. The turnip part that grows underground can be harvested at the same time as the turnip greens.

There are other root crops that can be included in a container garden such as ginger and taro, to name a few. Feel free to experiment with different cultivars that are recommended for containers. It can be an experience of a lifetime.

Supports and Trellises for Squash and Gourds

Vining crops such as gourds and squash can take up a considerable amount of space. Trellising is the wisest way to grow these types of vegetable in an urban garden. Saving space by growing upward allows the vines to produce effectively. It can be fun to create a framework to fit the allotted space. Imagine using sturdy dried bamboo stakes or recycled durable branches to form a frame. Think outside the box when imagining the possibilities. Worn-out tool handles can be painted, embellished with stone, or left in their natural state—all interesting options as garden supports. These are just a few of the possible items to consider when planning to build your own trellising.

The type of structure is important. When creating a trellis, good accessibility is essential, especially when harvesting. The crop should be easily accessible from as many sides as possible. Think about what the mature size of the crop will be. If the structure is not sturdy enough, the chance of collapsing is greatly increased. Make certain that the materials used are stable enough to last for the whole season and that they are durable enough to support the crop.

The weight of what is grown should be a consideration in deciding what is used to weave in and out for support. Twine is traditionally used for weaving a supporting grid. Consider using other non-traditional household materials as well. Items such as old T-shirts, worn sheets, and colorful heavyweight string are all alternative resources. Cutting an old T-shirt into strips is a terrific way to make fabric "string" at no cost.

Why throw out an old worn sheet, when it can be torn into strips and perhaps used as a sling? Heavier crops that would traditionally be grown on the ground can be supported by the grid if a sling or cradle is created. When creating a sling, the material used should be wider in the middle so that it can cover a broad area. This will equalize stress on the frame. The supporting grid should be woven in a way that supports the weight of the crop.

Consider how the grid will affect the care and harvest of the crop. A tightly woven grid can serve multiple duties. If the grid is tightly woven at the base, small nibblers will be discouraged. A tight weave will also help keep wayward stems tucked inside, keeping the crop within bounds. A loosely woven grid has multiple virtues too. A loose weave helps with air circulation. This helps with disease control. This type of support does provide better access for harvesting and does allow for growing sun-sensitive crops. One other benefit is the possibility of increasing the yield when harvesting the crop. The exterior and interior of a well-spaced grid gives double the surface area in less space.

Tap into your creative mind when considering a support or trellis in the garden. Eclectic structures can be fun and bring a smile—especially when using alternative materials for the framework or grid.

Growing Edible Herbs

Herbs are some of the easiest plants to grow. These plants can be used to season food and drinks through most seasons. Deciding on which herbs to grow should be based on what herbs you will be using regularly. Doing research into the herb's growth habits should also become a part of the decision about site selection. Herbs are easily grown in pots, window boxes, or even in the ground.

Herbs should be grown in full sun, have adequate air circulation, and should always be placed where they are most accessible. There are perennial herbs and annuals herbs. Consider growing a mixed pot or border of hardy perennials. As these herbs return year after year, give them a permanent spot in the garden. Most perennial herbs do not require rich soil. Well-drained, friable (crumbly) soil will enable the roots to produce a healthy plant.

Herbs in the mint family should always be contained in a pot where the roots are not allowed to escape. Escaped mints can quickly overpower the garden. Parsley, rosemary, lavender, and garlic chives are a few herbs commonly found in the perennial herb garden. Check the cold hardiness of rosemary and lavender to see if they are appropriate for your area.

Annual herbs are quite easy to grow in containers. A moderate-sized pot or window box can hold a variety of edible herbs. A good lightweight potting soil will provide the rooting conditions for the herbs to thrive. A regular but mild fertilization schedule will ensure your herbs are appropriately fed. Groupings of similar herbs can make quite a diverse collection. Try finding herbs with variegated, textured, or uniquely colored leaves to create a colorful culinary conversation.

If herbs are planted in pots, watering will be essential. Watering herbs at the base of the plant will help avoid fungal issues on the leaves—particularly if the environment is humid. Several herbs (such as thyme, oregano, and sage) like a Mediterranean climate. Sandy, well-draining, neutral soil will work best for these types of herb plants. Perhaps consider a drip irrigation system to connect the pots with similar watering needs. With emitters placed into each pot, these will be a handy way to water all your pots at once.

Regular pruning of herb plants is essential. Letting herbs grow without harvesting any leaves all season will shorten the life of the plant. Pruning encourages new growth and produces a stronger plant with a better branching structure. Some herbs, when they are allowed to flower, take this as a signal to stop growing. Basil is one example of this. Removing the flower heads will signal the herb to keep producing edible leaves.

A culinary herb garden within reach is an asset for any cook. Whether herbs are grown in a pot near the grill or reside in a container outside the kitchen door, herbs are an essential part of the garden.

Dwarf and Small Fruit Trees

Dwarf fruit trees are a great way to grow fruit in a limited space. The term "dwarf" is relative, of course. In this case, we are talking about trees that stay under 10 feet (3 m) tall. The top benefit of these small trees, aside from not taking up too much space, is that they keep their fruit within reach for easy picking.

Many dwarf fruit trees are container grown which helps to keep their growth in check. You will also need to do regular pruning and maintenance to ensure that they keep their small size and desired shape. Because they are container-grown, they will also need regular fertilizing and repotting once they outgrow their current home.

Being in a container has a side benefit of allowing the dwarf fruit tree to be mobile and can be moved inside your home, greenhouse, or other protected area during the wintertime. This means you can select a fruit that is not necessarily cold hardy in your planting zone. For that reason, many people that grow dwarf fruit trees keep them on a rolling trolley or use a base with wheels, so they can be more easily moved around.

Good choices for dwarf fruit trees include figs, citrus, and bush cherry. Fruit trees also require some extra upkeep. That can range from applying dormant sprays to hand-thinning the fruits, depending on the variety and type of tree that you choose.

Most fruit trees are grafted onto a "hardy" root stock—meaning that the tree's roots are a different variety than that which is growing above the graft point or node. This is done because the root stock can provide a healthy support system for a more delicate variety. You will need to note where that graft point is and look out for any growth that may come from below it. These can also be in the form of shoots or sprouts that pop up from the root zone. As soon as you see them, simply prune them off at or below ground level (as deep as you can). If you let them grow, they can sometimes take over the tree and dominate the plant. Then, you are left with a tree that bears different fruit (often inferior) than what you had originally purchased.

Another kind of grafting you see on some small and dwarf fruit trees involves single branches of different types of fruit that are grafted on the same plant. This can be done to create a tree with several different varieties on just one tree. For instance, an apple tree could have one branch that is 'Fuji' and another branch with 'Honeycrisp' apples growing on it. This can also be done with pear trees. It is a great way to have a whole orchard's worth of choices on only one tree or a few trees. There are also "fruit cocktail" trees that have different varieties of plums and peaches grafted on them. These franken-trees can be trained into a dwarf or columnar form. They can also be trained to grow flat along a wall or fence line. (See chapter 11 Vertical Growing Ideas for more information about growing and training Espalier trees flat against a wall.)

Cool-Season Edibles

Enjoying food from the garden at any time of the year is quite the experience. Enjoying cool-season edibles grown at home can be quite addictive. The urban garden offers a great setting for growing edibles that love it cool.

Preparing to plant cool-season annuals in a pot is quite easy. Clear the existing potting soil of all weeds and debris from the previous year's gardening activities. Add compost and sow seeds or plant young transplants, water well, and watch the planter come to life.

When growing directly in the ground, move back any straw or mulch. If the ground is not frozen, cultivate the existing soil and add compost. Cultivating the soil will allow the tender roots of the transplants to quickly take root and thrive. The decision about whether to sow seeds or source starter plants will depend on the time of year.

Cool-season edibles usually grow and produce when the temperatures are moderately cool, usually between 45°F to 75°F (7°C to 24°C). When sowing seeds, make certain the soil is friable and damp. If the soil is too wet, the seed will rot and not germinate. One of the easiest seeds to sow early (and often) is parsley.

Parsley needs about 100 days from germination to harvest. You could start it inside in the refrigerator to mimic nature's chilling hours. It is also easy to simply sow outside when the ground has thawed and is workable. It is best to sow these seeds weekly to have as much parsley as possible. Not all the seeds sown will germinate and germination takes a long time (2 to 6 weeks). Make sure to mark the area so it will not be disturbed as you continue to make use of the surrounding garden space.

Sowing lettuce is quite easy. There are many varieties of lettuce and every year more varieties are introduced. There are lettuces that are quite cold hardy and can be sown as early as possible. Some common varieties are leaf, bibb (butterhead), and heading lettuces such as 'Iceberg'. Sowing different varieties of lettuce offers diversity in the cool-season garden. Harvesting leaves from the different types sown can create a colorful salad plate.

Other cool-season crops to consider that can also be sown early are radishes, beets, spinach, and carrots. Beets offer a wonderful root crop, as well as tasty, edible leaves. Cooked or used raw in a salad, beets come in many colors and are very tasty when harvested fresh from the urban garden.

As the season progresses and temperatures climb, consider growing cabbage, broccoli, cauliflower, chard, or kohlrabi. There are many varieties of these cool-season vegetables. Grow the types you know you will eat or try something new. The cool-season garden offers the gardener time to experiment with easy, edible crops. Most cool-season crops do not take up a lot of space and are appealing in the late winter garden.

Berries and Fruits in Containers

Growing fruit in an urban setting is a great idea. There are many different options of what to grow, how to grow it, and what size container is required. With many new introductions every season, berries and small fruit bushes in containers can be quite exciting and rewarding.

Some smaller fruits, such as strawberries, can be overlooked when they are grown in the landscape. Growing these in a pot allows gardeners to grow abundant produce in a small space—and fruits and berries grown this way are easy to harvest. An 8- to 12-inch (20 to 30 cm) container can hold approximately ten plants. These small fruits are perennial, are shallow-rooted, and will multiply from runners. A creative way to grow strawberries is in containers with holes on the sides, in window boxes, or even in fabric containers. Given 8 hours of sun, in the right climate, and with ample water, strawberries are one of the easiest container fruits to grow.

Blueberries, gooseberries, and black currants are also easy to grow in the right containers. Many of the recently introduced cultivars are specifically bred for container growing. It is important to have enough room for the roots to grow comfortably so the plant can support its above ground growth. You will also need more than one plant to cross pollinate and ensure an abundant harvest. A container no smaller than 24 inches (60 cm) is perfect for growing these fruits. Each fruit will have different growing requirements. Blueberry bushes require acidic soil and full sun. They are beautiful when they are in bloom. After the blooms, the berries will need to be covered for protection from hungry birds.

A larger container will be required for growing blackberries and raspberries. These fruits can become invasive when planted in the ground.

In a large pot, growth can be easily controlled. These fruits are shallow-rooted and spread by underground runners. Full sun, compost, and ample water will allow these plants to thrive. Once the fruit has been harvested, cut the older canes down to the surface of the soil. For newer cultivars, the canes are generally upright and will not need support. On older raspberry types, new canes will need to be supported and staked. Once these canes touch the ground, they will root and grow.

Raspberries and blackberries are self-fertile. Usually, these fruits do not require more than one plant to produce fruits. However, with more plants, the yield is increased.

Figs are often overlooked as an option for growing a fruiting shrub in a pot. A 15- to 20-gallon (68 to 90 L) pot has more than enough room to allow a fig to grow. Depending on your climate, it is best to place this pot on casters. This will allow this plant to be moved to a protected place indoors, such as a garage, during the winter months, if required. Figs need a well-draining soil mix and a minimum of 6 hours of sun per day. Patience will be necessary as it might take a few years before fruiting starts. Once the fruits begin forming, protection from birds will be required.

Berries and fruiting bushes in containers allow the urban homeowner to have homegrown fruits in minimal space.

Trench Composting

One challenge many urban and small-space gardeners have is finding a place to compost the large quantity of weeds, trimmings, and other overgrowth they generate. One solution is to subscribe to a compost service, if you are fortunate enough to have one available locally. They will pick up your kitchen and garden scraps on a regular basis throughout the year and then deliver back to you a share of the beautiful compost that they have made from all their collections.

If a compost pick-up or subscription service is not in your area or out of reach of your budget, there are a variety of ways to deal with the extra plant material you have created. Trench composting is a tactic that farmers have been using for generations and this technique can be scaled down for small-space gardens as well.

Gardeners literally dig a trench about 1 to 3 feet (30 to 100 cm) deep and then put their scrapes into it. Make the trench as long or as wide/narrow as you want. Fill up the trench with your vegetable peelings, garden refuse, etc. and then cover the trench up loosely with soil and let it cook. The materials will decompose in the trench and will make an ideal growing bed for the next growing season. *Voila!* An instant raised bed garden.

Burying plant waste saves you the time and effort of working organic materials into the soil and supplies nutrients right at the root level for your plants. Native Americans used trench composting when they buried fish parts to fertilize their hills of corn. Rose gardeners have long talked about putting banana peels in the hole when they plant new bushes to give then a little boost.

An even simpler form of trench composting is putting plant refuse and food scraps in the bottom of a planting hole before you plant. To speed up the decomposition process, break down the plant materials first by cutting them into small pieces. In the kitchen, throw any cooking scraps into a blender and pour that slurry into your composting trench or freeze it until the soil is thawed and you can add it to your trench.

Trench composting also works when using large containers. And a side benefit of burying compost is that it keeps rodents and pests out of the compost pile. Further, decomposing food scraps underground means no smell above ground.

CHAPTER 4

Garden Entertaining

THE GARDEN IS a space to make your own, and of course to invite others in to enjoy it as well. Entertaining in the garden is a great way to welcome guests and share the fruits of your hard work. There are several options to consider to create a space that feels inviting. First, decide if you want a formal outdoor space or a more eclectic setting.

In an informal garden setting, think of ways to connect your visitors to the beauty which surrounds them. Consider bringing indoor conveniences into the garden. Excess items found around the home can come in quite handy when there is an immediate need for outdoor seating. Entertaining in the garden should be a memorable experience. Use your imagination and see how easy it is to make great entertaining happen in your garden.

Clever Seating Ideas

Gardeners get so preoccupied with filling every possible available spot with plants that we forget to put in a place to sit down. A gardener should never be so busy that they never get a chance to rest, relax, and enjoy the fruits of their labor.

Anything that safely supports your weight can be a seat. Garden containers of various kinds can serve as a resting spot. A sturdy board supported by two overturned buckets can make an impromptu sitting area or just the bucket itself will do sometimes.

A straw bale with a blanket thrown over it is an old-fashioned seating solution. If you use straw bales, they can be recycled in the garden for mulch or as a top-dressing.

Neatly stack several cinder (cement) blocks or bricks and throw a pillow on the top to make the seat more comfortable and you have a quick resting spot. Also, think about which natural materials you can use for seating, such as a tree stump or large rocks.

Indoor furniture repurposed for outdoor use works well too. Give them a new lease on life by stripping them down or painting them in new colors. Remember to coat wooden pieces with varnish so they can withstand the weather and elements.

Concrete is an inexpensive material to work with. It can be shaped and poured around objects and framed to create both seating and storage. In this clever example shown below, the urban gardeners have also formed a backing wall with a planting area in it. The cushions add an inviting touch.

This concrete bench is left with a raw finish, but it could also be easily painted or given a decorative coating. It can also be embellished with mosaic tile or have other objects affixed to the surface.

Seating possibilities using sculpting are almost limitless when dealing with concrete as you can shape the seating depth and storage openings to your exact specifications. The effect is quite primitive and modern at the same time.

Tablescapes

Make your garden guests feel welcome and special by setting out a beautiful tablescape for them in your garden. This display establishes a feeling of hospitality and creates the mood for their visit.

A tablescape can be left out as a permanent part of your seasonal décor or be made to last just for the duration of your event. The display can be on a dining table, a potting bench, or any surface that is open, even, and flat.

Complete settings are nice, but matching plates and cups are unnecessary. Collect dishware in the same color family or style and group them as you like. Your style might be formal or casual, classic or modern.

Adding a pretty tablecloth, runner, and napkins softens the scene and brings a note of grace to the garden. Look for cloths made out of weatherproof materials that can be left outside and will not fade or be damaged when they get wet. Layering your cloths makes for any even more interesting and nuanced display.

Place a vase full of blooms or a flowering plant in a pot as the centerpiece of the tablescape. Alternatively, place a group of small pots or vases down the middle of the table or put one at each place setting. Votives, large candles in glass jars, or hurricane candle lamps can be lit as dusk approaches for a flattering glow.

Use natural elements from your garden or travels to decorate as well. Cut branches placed down the center of the table or between each place setting will make a dramatic impact. Use natural items such as coral picked up from a beach trip, or pinecones, pretty rocks, and dried seed heads collected from the garden. Place these natural elements in a large urn or open bowl for a striking effect. Look in your vegetable and herb garden for any bounty that you can harvest and display as well.

The tablescape need not include place settings for a formal lunch or dinner. It can be as simple as a bottle of water or wine and a few glasses placed on a metal tray. A bowl of fruit or nuts set out is another charming touch. Anything that conveys that you have thought of your guest's comfort will do.

The tablescape also doesn't have to be "real." You can set up a doll's tea party or a scene from a favorite novel or movie. Have fun arranging a vignette for your gathering friends and the fairies alike.

Hanging Wall Décor

Walls can often seem rather dull. Consider creating excitement with splashes of color using plants and pots. When adding hanging décor to walls consider the composition of the wall. Brick walls will need sturdy anchors installed. Wooden walls require supports that will hold the weight of the container in addition to the weight of the wet soil. Some walls will allow for more creative options that can be quite fun.

On a brick wall, hanging pots will add interest in any season, even when unplanted. If a conservative tone is desired, hanging urns could be considered wall art. During the winter months, adding greenery and berries sets a festive tone. A trailing evergreen plant adds a formal, yet unexpected, touch of softness. In lieu of urns, pots in basic black or white are also a creative twist—moving away from the traditional terra cotta pot.

Wooden walls and fences are often more flexible to use when considering hanging elements. Like a living room wall, hanging décor can be quite personal. Attaching shelving or shadow boxes allows small pots or containers to be utilized. A wooden wall behind a cottage garden might have a shelf or hooks to put up a few wired vases. Gracefully scattered on the wall, this is a perfect way to capture small blooms that might otherwise go unnoticed. Succulents planted in pitchers make a statement and create an eye-level floral conversation.

Adding found objects personalizes any wall. Consider creating a wall of found objects like the tines from a tiller, bike tire rims, or even garden tools that are no longer used—all painted in bright colors. Bicycle tire rims make a perfect floating work of art when they are hung mid-height with wire. The tire rims can even be attached to string anchored in the ground for the vine of your choice to climb. Wrapping the vine throughout the season creates a whimsical floral display that pops with color.

Fencing that is meant to remain semi-transparent offers some creative alternatives. If a wire fence is used, consider moss pockets as an option. In sunny areas, a moss-planted pocket is the perfect place for shallow-rooted succulents. If large enough, line the moss with sheets of newspaper to keep moisture in the root zone. Adding colorful plants in these pockets makes them appear to be floating in mid-air. Felt or fabric planting pockets on a wall can also be an option if the space is small. Hanging pots and *objets d'art* adds to the ambiance of the urban garden.

Consider hanging lightweight indoor plants from the underside of a patio umbrella. Houseplants of all types are terrific for this idea. Small plants in creative lightweight containers, such as jars, can be hung with festive macrame hangers—adding a fun touch to any patio or terrace. Using a string of outdoor lights will highlight these plants and add some classy whimsy as well. Creativity on your walls adds a personal touch and makes the space uniquely your own.

Glamping in the Garden

Our urban gardens are sometimes taken for granted. We work long hours in them and then we leave to go camping. On other occasions, we invite others to enjoy the urban garden beauty that we have created—and we work hard to entertain them. One way for us to *really* enjoy the outdoor spaces we love so well is by staying home and glamping.

Why go to a campsite and do without the niceties of home? Glamping in our own backyards is the answer—done with a twist. Utilizing all the creature comforts of being at home, while camping, can make for a memorable weekend. When considering the art of successful glamping, ambient lighting plays a big part. This doesn't necessarily have to be a campfire, but consider utilizing stowed away lamps, string lighting, or even large outdoor candles. Setting up clusters of candles can set a very romantic mood. To set the mood and create a defined area, use minimal lighting near a sitting area by perhaps stringing lights throughout the canopy of small trees or draping the lights over shrubs. An old lamp or two can also create an outdoor living room effect. Add a sleeping bag or small tent and it becomes an instant bedroom. Allow the imagination to flow and you have got a glamping weekend.

If you are inviting guests over, consider using empty canning jars, or clay pots to light the way. Fill the jars three-quarters full with a layer of sand or a soil and sand mix. Place votives or short candles inside the jars or pots. Light them just before dusk so they add subtle lighting along the walkway. These little spots of light can also highlight some extra special views in the garden.

Find the pillows that are unused from inside the house and bring them outdoors. Scattering them throughout the garden will create mini conversation areas. If you can find empty 5-gallon (23 L) buckets with lids, put a pillow on top of the lids and you have an improvised, comfortable, portable seating area that can be moved throughout the glamping area. Having extra seats that can accommodate a larger group is always advised. A glamping weekend will encourage your neighbors to visit and enjoy your garden with you.

Providing creative vessels for libations can also add a touch of charm to the evening. Consider upcycling empty canning jars. Canning jars can prove to be quite useful when glamping.

Why is the cooler only taken outside for picnics or large gatherings? Bring out the cooler instead of a beverage cart. Allow your guests to mix and pour their own drinks by having the ingredients on ice in the cooler. Consider chilling wine in a clean 5-gallon (23 L) bucket draped in a colorful linen and filled with ice. Tuck in bottles of white, rosé, and red wine for the appropriate chilling time, so your guests can choose their favorite and enjoy.

Make sure to consider easy serving options. Afterall, glamping should include relaxing while entertaining. Use skewers for your protein and vegetable food choices. Mix it up with unexpected fruits and fire them up on the grill. Serve everything on those platters that are inside, unused, and on the top shelf of the cabinet. Why keep saving them for a special occasion? Every day is special now—put those platters to good use.

Any day is the best day to go glamping in your urban garden. Entertaining and enjoying an urban garden is easier than you think.

Fire Pits

Fire pits are useful when entertaining friends and family. Having an outdoor heating source adds ambiance and creates an exciting reason to gather, even when the temperatures drop. Fire pits come in various forms. With a big enough yard and some creativity, you could even construct your own freestanding fire pit. When you incorporate a fire pit into the landscape, make certain the flames can be quickly contained.

Fire pits are sometimes embedded in tables. They are required to be positioned away from the house and surrounded by flame-resistant tiles. The homeowner needs to check the local fire ordinances, to determine what the law is regarding backyard open fires. This will vary with each jurisdiction. Generally, fire pits need to be at least 10 feet (3 m) away from any permanent structure. Look up for overhanging branches that might become a hazard if they catch fire. Keep all surrounding foliage moist, on the perimeter, and well away from the fire. If there is seating around the fire pit table, make certain all fabrics are flame retardant. The fire pit table should also have a covering over the flame area. This will minimize the chance of foreign objects dropping in and then becoming a flying fire hazard. Allowing adequate space between the edges of the table and the actual flame is important for the safe enjoyment of a fire pit table. Keep water nearby as a safety precaution.

Freestanding fire pits offer a safer alternative. Placing these pits in the lawn or away from heavily traveled pathways is key. Providing a sandpit around the fire pit is an increased safety option and an easy one to build. Whether you choose a square or rectangle sandpit this is also a good way to utilize unused space. A brick terrace or area with pavers is a good way to create a permanent spot for the freestanding fire pit. Centering the fire pit and adding safely distanced chairs will set the mood for a safe gathering.

Fire pits can be built in the ground as well. For a finished touch, purchase a metal fire pit bowl. To build your own fire pit, first define the size. Outline the area with spray paint. Dig down 6 inches (15 cm) to create the base. Remove the garden debris and place gravel in the hole. Add the first layer of block, brick, or stone. At this point you can insert the purchased fire ring or fire pit bowl to make certain that the base layer is level. For a higher fire pit, add additional layers. Remove the ring or bowl and stack up another layer of blocks or bricks, adding a fire-retardant adhesive as you place them in a staggered design. In-ground fire pits should be kept to a height that offers the best enjoyment for all family and friends. Make certain these in-ground fire pits are cleaned out from time to time, so the ashes don't accumulate and damage the fire pit.

Fire pits can be enjoyed no matter which kind you decide to include in your outdoor living space. They offer a unique way to encourage gathering outdoors safely.

Inviting Doorways and Entryways

A well-curated porch or doorway planting is an inviting (and essential) way to greet the visitors to your garden. They say first impressions are lasting ones and that's true of those your visitors form at the main entrance of your home or garden.

The style of your entry and porch area should be consistent with your home's architecture as well as your garden style. If you are a formal gardener, this might consist of an urn on each side of the door with a simple plant palette such as geraniums and ivy. If you are more of an informal gardener, this could be a looser collection of several containers with various kinds of plants.

Your entryway garden need not be static. You can change it each season or with each holiday. A low-maintenance technique to handle the seasonal transitions is to plant an evergreen shrub in a large pot and then surround the evergreen with different annuals appropriate for each season. For example, you can plant pansies and violas in the cool seasons and then petunias or verbena in the warm season.

Other quick seasonal switch-outs could include changing your door mat, the pillows on your porch furniture, and the hanging wreath or sign on your front door. A large bowl of objects placed on a nearby table can be a fun spot to share seasonal collections such as gourds and seashells.

It is always nice to provide entryway seating— if you have the room to do so. Even a small stool or bench can be a gracious touch for anyone carrying heavy packages or needing to rest for a minute upon arrival.

Along with your container plantings, you can add in pieces of art and other garden accents. These can be tucked in and among your pots, but should not be a trip hazard or be so cluttered as to block easy access to the door.

Look up as well. Is your house number clearly visible? Is the porch lighting fixture working and unobstructed? Is your door handle, bell, or knocker in working order? It might be time to upgrade or repair these for better first impression.

If your entryway or porch has a roof or overhang, a lovely touch is to paint the underside of it in a pale blue tone to mimic the sky. You can also consider adding hanging baskets to highlight the porch's columns or archways.

One additional tip is to think about changing the color of your door (if you are permitted to do so). A fresh coat of paint in a bright or dramatic color can have a huge impact on the look of your entryway and create a charming effect.

CHAPTER 5

Intensive Gardening for Small Spaces

NTENSIVE GARDENING MEANS using the resources you have to the fullest—gardening that capitalizes on results over effort. This section teaches you how to garden smarter, not harder. When we (at least most of us) first start out gardening, we tend to want to stuff it all—plants and containers and trellises—into the garden and maximize the growing space we have. In doing this we end up tackling too many projects all at once. Learning to use restraint is hard.

There are so many things that we should be paying attention to in the garden, it can be overwhelming. The following ideas for intensive gardening should be taken on one at a time. Implement one technique each year over several years. Once conquered, take on the next technique. Whether you are new to growing or a veteran gardener, we hope these tips teach you something new and save you from some wasted labor in the future.

Layered Plantings to Maximize Harvests

It is possible to have as robust a harvest from a small space by layering your plantings as you would have in a one-layer garden space that is two to three times the size. Layered edible beds are also called *intercropping*. A classic example is growing strawberry plants underneath asparagus in the same bed. These are both perennial crops, but they are harvested in different seasons and grow differently— using different spaces.

When layering crops, be aware that the taller plants may shade out the lower ones. This can be an advantage when trying to grow a vegetable that prefers cooler weather or having a taller one that thrives during your hot season. For instance, cabbages and other greens might be beneficially shaded by okra or pepper plants.

You may be familiar with the classic Three Sisters Garden used by the Native Americans. In this layered method, corn is planted in a cultivated soil mound. Beans are planted around the base of the corn so they can climb up the tall stalks. Then squash is planted to spread over the base of the mound. Employ this same layering technique by planting a tall crop, a climbing one, and a spreading one together in a container or raised bed.

Layering leafy herbs, such as parsley and cilantro, amongst rows of leeks, onions, and garlic can also work, though the edible bulbs may not grow as large and be as robust as if they had the soil and all its nutrients just for themselves.

Note also that plant labels and seed packs give optimal spacings that are just guidelines (and are not written in stone). Here is where a little experimentation can come into play. Often, plants are just as healthy and productive if they are planted at less than half the distance a plant tag might recommend them to be spaced at—some are fine even planted side-by-side.

If you are fine with harvesting some edible plants at their smaller or younger stages, you can place them a great deal closer than what the seed packs recommend. Baby carrots and arugula are good examples of this.

Carrots also work well combined with radishes in garden beds. They combine well together because radishes are a very fast crop to grow, and carrots take several weeks longer to germinate and mature. By the time you are harvesting your radishes, the carrot seedlings will appear and can expand into the empty space left by the radishes.

Succession Planting in the Edible Garden

Similar to layered plantings that increase harvests in a small space, succession planting deals with maximizing edible crops over the course of a set period of time in the edible garden—be that one growing season or a year or more.

Succession planting is the technique of planting one crop right after another. When one bed or container is harvested, you seed or plant seedlings of a new crop. Depending on your location, this can extend your growing season from early spring through late fall, and even through the winter in milder climates. An example of a succession planting for a small, raised bed space (or larger container) might be growing spinach in early spring, followed by bush beans in summer, and then broccoli in fall.

Note that determinate crops work best for succession planting—meaning edible plants that mature and are harvested pretty much all at once. Indeterminate vegetables such as pole beans and cucumbers will continue to produce a few fruits on and off all growing season long.

Many small-space gardeners also employ a related technique called *relay cropping*. With this you plant one short row of lettuce seeds at the start of the spring season, then plant a second row 2 to 3 weeks later, and a third row a few weeks after that. As the third row is going in, you can harvest the first planting of lettuce and so on. This spreads out your harvest to the rate you likely will be consuming them at, rather than having to process several pounds of greens all at once.

Succession planting takes some planning and thinking ahead to the next crop you will be planting in a given spot. An added wrinkle is the need to do crop rotation. You may not always be able to ensure that you are not placing the same member of an edible plant family in the same bed or container from year-to-year, but you can strive to do so by keeping careful records.

It's a good idea to install a cover crop or a thick layer of mulch sometimes between these successive plantings to allow the soil to recover. Mix in organic amendments such as alfalfa meal, aged manures, and fish fertilizer as well, so you are not over depleting the nutrients in your planting beds.

Patchwork Pavers

Pavers laid out in a checkerboard pattern will make a small space feel dynamic. Also known as patchwork pavers, this checkerboard technique is ideal for a small patch of lawn or to liven up a rooftop or terrace. The resulting effect mimics a checker board made with living carpet and is always a conversation starter.

Having some pavers in your garden (instead of an expanse of lawn) gives you a spot to step on that is not muddy and lets you set your chairs and pots on a firm, level surface that won't sink. This paving method also saves money as you do not need to purchase as many pavers to cover your total area.

The pattern of pavers can be a checkerboard design—skipping every other space and alternating

each row. Alternatively, the pavers and green spaces can be mixed more naturally for a patchwork quilt effect. The key is that the pavers be square and identical in size.

The growing areas between the pavers can be turfgrass, moss, or any steppable groundcover, such as these tough sedums shown here. In this example, the pavers are on top of a garage space that is converted into a garden area overlooking a back alley.

To build a checkerboard paver pattern, first start with a level area. If the area is already planted, excavate it out, measure the space and mark out the paver spacing. At each paver location, fill in the paver base area with fine sand and tamp it down.

Then place the paver on the sand base and use a bubble level to make sure it is level. After all the pavers are placed, fill the remaining spaces with topsoil, and plant your lawn or groundcover between them.

If you are up for a challenge, you might mix in two or three different kinds of the same type of groundcover into the pattern. For instance, use a light green moss and a dark green one to create even greater visual interest.

Gravel can be used to alternate between planted areas and pavers for an additional textural element. Synthetic turf cut in squares is another filler alternative if turfgrass is difficult to grow in your climate.

Small Trees and Trees in Containers

Trees are often the last thing a new small-space gardener thinks to add to their landscape. After all, trees grow large and take up valuable growing space. We would rather use all that precious garden real estate for growing sun-loving flowers, herbs, and vegetables.

However, trees should be among your first considerations when planning your small-space garden. And yes, no matter how small your space is, you can fit in a small tree. Small trees are those that grow to be less than 25 feet (7.5 m) high. Trees can be container grown and root-pruned to force them to stay small. There are also dwarf and miniature types of trees for exceedingly small spaces.

The shape of the tree can also determine its placement and usage. There are trees that are bred to be columnar or very narrow in their growth habit, as well as those that branch out at a great height, so they do not interfere with lower-level plantings. Trees that grow in a weeping habit are a terrific option for small spaces as the branches hang down from the top of the tree and stay in a fairly contained area.

Shade in the garden is often underrated. After a few months of gardening (in any climate), you will wake up one day and realize you no longer want to be out in the direct sun all day, every day. This is where a nice small shade tree can have its place in the garden. If you have set up a small seating area, you will want to place the tree in the southwest corner of the area to maximize the shade coverage there.

In general, deciduous trees (those that lose their leaves in winter) are a better choice for small-space gardens as they can provide shelter in summer and then let in sunlight through their bare branches in the winter when the days are shortest.

When looking for a specimen tree, you might evaluate your choices by your answers to the following questions: Do you want a tree that flowers for a long or short period of time? Do you want a fruit-bearing tree? Do you want a tree with colorful or variegated foliage? Do you want a tree that supports native wildlife? Do you want a tree that is sterile and does not aggravate pollen allergies? The answers to these questions will help you choose a tree that has many of these benefits or that has just one or two of them.

Trees that are container grown need more nutrients than those planted in a garden bed, so you will need to fertilize them regularly. Every few years, you will also have to remove the tree from its container and upgrade the tree to a slightly larger container, adding in fresh soil as well.

Trees should not be treated like furniture. They will need care. Once planted, they will need regular watering and occasional pruning. You will need to rake up any dropped leaves, flowers, seed pods, nuts, or fruits—these can all be added to your compost pile, another side benefit to having trees.

Groundcovers as Lawn Alternatives

A turfgrass lawn can have its place in a landscape, say as a play area for children or an exercise space for adults. The lawn can also be used as an open area countering effect to create a visual relief from busy garden beds and borders.

However, a grass lawn can also be the highest maintenance area of your garden. It requires weekly (or more often) mowing during the growing season, along with regular reseeding, fertilizing, watering, etc. Depending on what area you live in, turfgrass can also be an environmental liability either for its intensive use of resources (water, fertilizer, fuel, etc.) or by causing stormwater runoff issues due to its lack of quick rain absorption in comparison to other plantings.

If you are not going to use an open area for constant activity, consider using other groundcover plants in place of turfgrass. Many of the ground-cover choices available are selected and marketed as "steppable" in that they can take light foot traffic. These groundcovers are great choices in areas that you may step into occasionally. These can include carex (sedges), low-growing succulents, and miniature or creeping varieties of herbs.

Other areas of your landscape may not be hospitable to a turfgrass lawn as they are too shady or wet. In those cases, consider a moss lawn or other shade-loving groundcover. Moss lawns are a particularly attractive alternative that not only are beautiful but can tolerate moderate foot traffic.

Groundcovers can also be used under trees and around shrubs where you do not want to take a chance interfering with the plant roots. The plants act as a living green mulch and save you the trouble of adding and regularly reapplying mulch around those areas. Good choices for this use of groundcovers include shorter perennials that are fast spreading, such as bugleweed (*Ajuga* sp.) and barrenwort (*Epimedium* sp.). Look also for native groundcover plants suitable to your location that can naturalize and form a nice, thick planting.

In the hot and sunny spots of your landscape, you might find it hard to get many plants to fill in under these harsh conditions. Those spots are perfect for the Mediterranean herbs such as lavender, santolina, or sage. This category of plants enjoys being out in the heat and being planted in well-draining soils.

One caveat with groundcovers in general is that when you first plant them, you will be hoping they will spread and fill in the space quickly. Then a few years down the road, you might wish these plants were not so aggressive in their growth habit. That is the nature of the beast. Know that it will take them a couple of years to settle in, establish their root systems, and then they will take off. After the third year or so, you will need to selectively thin or dig out any errant plants that are encroaching in spaces you do not want them to go. At that point, you can start sharing those excess groundcover plants with friends and neighbors.

Keeping a Garden Journal and Organized Plant Records

Keeping your garden records organized is one of the best ways to ensure you have success. This can be in the form of a garden journal, a spreadsheet on your computer, or as simple as a shoebox that holds all your paper records.

By keeping track of your progress from year-to-year you'll have a record you can constantly refer to when planning your future garden. One of the many joys of gardening is looking back and seeing the progress that has been made. Starting from a barren weedy lot and progressing to perennial beds bursting with color, you can be proud of that transition and how much you have grown—both literally and figuratively!

An easy way to keep track is with a blank notebook or three-ring binder. Go bigger than you think you will need as you will be surprised by how much information and the number of details you want to save in your garden journal.

The first thing you will want to do is make a sketch of your garden layout. You can do this on graph paper or print a photo of your space and draw directly on it. Next, mark out what plantings are currently there and then add in new planting areas that you want to put in during the next season (or the season thereafter).

Remember this is all planning for years to come; don't think you need to do it all at once! A good principle is to tackle one major project each year and pace yourself as you go. But don't let that stop you from dreaming! This journal is a place to put down all your possibilities. Start a page for plants you want to grow, design ideas you want to use, and other garden inspirations you come across. Cut out plants, pictures, and articles and paste them into your wish list pages.

In the journal or wherever you store your plant records, add sections for seed packs, plant tags, and online purchase orders. Have a chart of general gardening information for your area. List your hardiness zone, first and last average frost dates, soil test results, and anything else you will be referring to frequently. Make a page for each month of the year and what garden tasks need to be done during that period. Add in tasks and reminders—when a shrub is pruned, when your garlic is ready to harvest, etc.

Don't forget to set some pages aside for wildlife sightings and drawings. You can start a section for noting what insects visit and when they arrive as well. Take notes on unusual weather occurrences and firsts in your garden (for example, your earliest pea harvest, biggest zinnia blooms, etc.).

Dedicate a half-hour or so each week during the growing season to keeping your journal or plant records updated. Then plan to spend a cold winter's evening going back over your garden journals or plant records, not just as a planning tool for the next growing season, but also for the sheer enjoyment of it.

Grouping Plants by Lighting Needs

For every light level in the garden, there are plants that have been bred for that location. Knowing how much light is required for a specific plant to thrive is important. Matching the garden lighting to the right plant is a key component in having a healthy plant. The first step is learning what type of lighting is in the garden. Think of the garden as having different lighting zones.

Full sun would be the first zone. This is an area where plants capable of handling as much sun and heat as possible would thrive. Usually in full sun areas, there is minimal to no shade present to shield these plants from the direct sun. Reading the plant tag will tell you whether the plant will thrive under these conditions. The best plant selections in this full sun zone are often tropical or extra durable, tough annuals or perennials. Usually, this zone would receive more than 6 hours of full sun during the day. Rudbeckia, hibiscus, roses, and ornamental grasses usually fall into this lighting zone.

Part-sun plantings commonly receive between 4 to 6 hours of sun per day. The shadow cast by nearby houses or even the overhead tree canopy can often offer protection in these part-sun plantings. This lighting zone offers a vast array of plant choices. In this zone there will be areas that receive more sun than shade, which is perfect for plants that might be sun lovers. Often even the sun-loving plants will need a little bit of a break from the sun's direct rays. Plantings in this lighting zone will vary in the length of sun exposure they receive. Knowing the required sun exposure is important. Echinacea, bluebeard (*Caryopteris* cvs.), baptisia, and hydrangea fall under this category.

Shade plantings usually receive less than 4 hours of sun each day. Nestled under the canopy of trees, or on the shady side of the house, these plants thrive under sheltered conditions. The early morning sun is fine and helps these plants enjoy some light but they cannot tolerate the strong rays of the midday sun that can harm leaves or excessively dry out the soil. Some plants which fall under this category are the hostas, azaleas, and rhododendrons, to name a few.

Dappled shade plantings usually struggle with sun exposure but thrive under the shadows. Sunlight gently peeking through the canopy of a woodland could be considered another lighting zone. These plants require only a hint of sun which means their environment is cool and often moist. Plant options for this lighting zone could include columbine (*Aquilegia*), coral bells (*Heuchera*), lady's mantle (*Alchemilla*), and spotted dead nettle (*Lamium*) cultivars.

When considering what level of lighting you have in the garden, take time to observe the space, and consider the appropriate plant. You will notice the light levels will change at different times of the day. With each season, the lighting in the garden will vary depending on the density of the tree canopy, the positioning of the sun, and more. Investing time in knowing where the lighting zones are found and what you are able to grow in the garden is a financially sound idea.

Grouping Plants by Watering Needs

Plant health and maintenance in the urban garden is simple if you think of each area as a community. Each community will have different needs. Grouping plants together by what is required to keep them hydrated is an important part of plant health.

Site selection is the first step in building a thriving and healthy plant community. Successfully managing a full-sun site will involve selecting plants that are appropriate to the site conditions. A garden site that has full sun and will get minimal hydration will be perfect for plants that can tolerate hot, dry, well-draining sites. The perimeter of the garden might be just this type of site. Plants that would fall into this full-sun and minimal-watering category could also be placed in an area that is out of the way such as in the rear of the yard or in an area that is infrequently visited.

Plants that require a moderate level of hydration should be placed where they can be watered when required. The middle of the garden is optimal for this. Finding a location that receives a balance of sun and shade will help keep plants with moderate

watering needs happy together. Watering these plants once a week will usually keep them healthy. The shade will help keep the soil moist, so these plants do not dry out quite so fast.

A plant under stress will show decline quickly. Noticing the signs of stress can help save a plant. The signs of plant stress are when leaves begin to drop, yellow, or curl. Addressing symptoms before it gets too late is important. Check to see if the ground is too moist or not draining properly. If it is too wet, the plant might show signs of rotting roots or leaf or stem diseases. Consider watering only when the soil is dry. Insert your index finger into the top 2 inches (5 cm) of the soil. If it is dry, water deeply. If the soil is moist, delay watering for a day or two, unless extreme temperatures or excessive winds dictate otherwise.

Plants that require an abundance of water should be placed near an outside hose spigot. These plants would benefit from being planted in a low-lying area of the garden. Usually a swale, a slightly depressed area of the garden, is perfect for plants in this watering category. As these plants thrive on wet feet, creating an area where the water might puddle will serve this purpose. While drainage might not be essential, the water should drain sufficiently enough to avoid root rotting.

Healthy plants that have compatible requirements are an asset to any garden. Selecting plants with the best fit for the site, the watering needs, as well as the feeding needs, will help keep the garden in tip-top shape. Communities where plants thrive and complement each other start with a healthy, hydrated environment.

Raised Beds and Square Foot Gardens

Raised beds and square foot gardens can create beautiful areas for planting within the urban garden. Traditionally these types of gardens were placed in the backyard. As neighborhoods have changed, now artfully curated raised beds can also be found in the front yard. It is merely a matter of aesthetics and what your community will allow.

Raised beds allow for earlier planting of the garden in the spring. These types of beds thaw out and warm up quickly in the springtime. Selecting the materials for the raised bed can be quite the adventure. Creative use of untreated lumber, bricks, wine bottles, and other repurposed materials are often used to build raised beds. The soil should be a minimum of 8 inches (20 cm) deep. Harvesting produce from a raised bed should be easily accessible when reaching in from most of the sides. The optimum width is 4 feet (1.2 m) for ease of maintenance. The length can vary depending on the space where the garden is installed.

Adding the proper soil amendments for optimum plant growth is crucial. Existing garden soil is often too dense for many plants. Lightening up the soil with additional natural soil amendments will help the roots grow down into the soil and support plant health. Incorporating items such as shredded leaves, grass clippings, humus, and manure will aid in building a fluffy, nutrient-rich soil.

Raised beds often include a diverse collection of plants. They are not always used just for growing edibles. Raised beds can contain plants that encourage pollinating insects and wildlife visits. Some urban gardens incorporate a mix of edible plants as well as flowers simply to have some for cutting and sharing.

Square foot gardens, if planted properly, offer maximum harvest in a smaller, organized space. Long beds, no more than 4 feet (1.2 m) wide are

the recommended specifications for a square foot garden. The size and width of a traditional square foot garden allows for reaching in and harvesting from all sides. Walking in a square foot garden is not recommended.

The principles of square foot gardening are quite simple. First a square grid must be built to fit the space. Usually, the squares are 1 foot x 1 foot (30 x 30 cm) in size. Planting intensively in the grid squares (and not in rows) can reduce weeding. This decreases the amount of exposed soil that allows weeds to take root.

Compost, peat moss, and vermiculite are recommended for the square foot garden. This soil mixture stays loose and fluffy. It is recommended that each square be planted with various amounts of plants depending on the type being grown. For example, one squash plant in a square will fill the entire space upon maturity. Realistically one pepper plant can be grown in a square and eight to ten bush beans. After harvesting the square, add more compost and replant with another crop. Keeping a journal of what is planted in each square is very important. It is amazing how much can be grown in a simple square foot garden.

Observing the lighting of the new garden space and deciding what to plant are the beginning of the raised bed planting journey. Committing to a square foot garden bed is an adventure in maximizing yield in a contained area. Each of these concepts offer a great learning experience for urban gardeners.

Weed Suppression Techniques

Weeds don't care if your garden is in the city or the country. They are equal opportunity offenders. Weeds can sneak into any pot or empty garden spot. The second a gardener turns their back, they appear. It is important to be proactive and get ahead of removing weeds.

Basic weed suppression methods include exclusion and smothering. In other words, laying down a material that will block weed seeds from germinating or stop underground runners from emerging in an area. Garden supply stores sell weed-blocking materials (also known as landscape cloth or fabric). This material allows water and air to permeate, but prevents most sunlight or anything else to get through it. You can also use other repurposed materials to block weeds such as old carpeting or burlap, but this kind of weed block is best used under garden furniture and pathway areas. It should not be placed over tree roots.

After weed-blocking material, a thick layer of mulch is your next best defense. Mulches include

bark chips, pine straw, shredded leaves, and various stages of composted plant material. These will break down after a few months and work their way into the soil, adding nutrients and beneficial organic materials. Mulches also provide the additional benefits of regulating the soil temperature and moisture levels.

For an additional layer of weed suppression defense, put down a thick layer of newspaper, then wet it down before you mulch an area. Newspaper is made from wood pulp and will break down quickly under the mulch. Similarly, brown paper grocery bags cut open and laid out also make a good base layer for weed suppression.

You can even plant a living mulch to suppress weeds by growing a thick groundcover under taller plantings or in a weed-prone open area of your garden. Groundcovers work best when planted close together to form a thick, green carpet that prevents weeds from getting a toehold. Fair warning though, many plants categorized as groundcovers are aggressive spreaders and need to be contained and kept in-bounds lest they march all over the rest of your garden.

This living or "green" mulch might be seasonal—also referred to as a cover crop. Cover crops literally cover the ground between your growing seasons. They can even add nutrients back into the soil during this fallow period by fixing nitrogen and holding it at the root level (as many members of the legume family do, such as field peas and crimson clover). You then turn over or chop these cover crops off at the soil level and let the roots decay in place. This will help prepare your bed for the next planting season.

CHAPTER 6

Gardening Styles for Small Spaces

THIS NEXT SECTION of the book describes various classic garden styles that can be applied to small spaces. Selecting an overall garden style will help focus your efforts. Embracing a theme will save you from wasting resources and time as the boundaries of the style you choose will guide many of the decisions you make.

You may also want to have designated spaces in your garden with different garden styles and purposes—also known as garden rooms. Separate your garden rooms with visual cues that you are entering a new area. These dividers can be fixed or moveable, such as planted hedges, a row of tall containers, or a piece of large outdoor furniture. Another way to indicate a transition from one garden room to another is a change in paving, surfaces, or elevation—done by stepping up or down.

Combining garden styles is certainly an option and a great way to personalize your space. For instance, try combining a shade garden with a habitat style. Whatever style you choose, interpret it any way your heart desires and make it your own.

Night Garden or a Moon Garden

If you work outside the home, you might only get to enjoy your garden during the day on the weekend or on holidays. A night garden (also known as a moon garden) can open up a whole new way of enjoying your landscape after dark. Once your eyes have adjusted to the lower light levels, a different world opens up.

Night gardens are also wonderful for entertaining. Place a few candles around in glass hurricane lamps or light a few lanterns to create an enchanting and mysterious atmosphere. Strings of lights always add a festive and inviting touch.

The city lights are often enough to see your way safely, but if you are worried about guests navigating a winding pathway you can add a few solar lights at strategic spots around your landscape.

Sitting out in the garden after the sun goes down is an experience that few people really take advantage of to the fullest. There are many benefits to a night garden stroll. It is cooler in the summer and the insects are less active.

You will want to take note of where in your garden it is brighter at night and where the full moon's glow might be best seen. A night garden can be designed around a small seating area or viewing spot just for this purpose.

Plant choices for night or moon gardens include any white or pale flowers that stay open after dusk. There are also a few plants with blooms that only up at night. They include moonflower, night-blooming jasmine, evening primrose, and tuberose.

Next, you will want to select plants with foliage that is variegated or has a silvery finish as it shines nicely under the moonlight. These include many kinds of hosta, heuchera, caladium, and brunnera.

Then, you can start playing with hardscaping and other surfaces to add visual interest to the moon or night garden. For example, you can use tables with mirrored tops or mirror trays set upon them. Pillows can be made reflective with sequin trims and beading. White rocks can outline a path. Metal or white containers can hold plantings at various heights.

Sound is also an essential part of the night garden. As you rely less on your eyesight, your other senses become keener. A bubbling water feature nearby is a soothing touch, as is a small wind chime. The rustling of the breeze in tall grasses or bamboo is another pleasant night-time experience.

Finally, set up a comfortable seating area with a few blanket throws and place a chiminea, fire pit, or outdoor gas fireplace at its heart to enjoy the garden on cooler nights.

Japanese Style or an Asian-Themed Garden

Asian-themed gardens can make a space in the urban garden quite peaceful. There is something about being mindful and creating a restful spot right outside the door. These gardens have a few elements that are consistently found in Asian-themed gardens and can be expressed in creative ways.

A water element is commonly included in an Asian-themed garden. When thinking of a water element, it can be as simple as a softly dripping fountain. Perhaps a small recirculating trickle of water is flowing over a streambed made of river rock. The subtle water sound can be a masking effect that drowns out distracting noise from beyond the garden. A basin filled with a puddle of water that has a few petals from nearby flowers also creates a calming scene. There is also a way to include a dry, water-like effect in this type of garden. Using small, crushed gravel or sand, a raked area can mimic a water-like feature.

Stone is another mainstay of the Asian-themed garden. Stone and large rocks are the typical natural hardscaping and considered the backbones of the garden. Large, smooth rocks can be used for additional seating in secluded nooks within the garden. A solitary rock by a water feature can be considered a grounding feature. When rocks with distinctive characteristics are used, they become elegant additions to the garden, even if they are merely decoration.

Pathways gently escort guests deeper into the serene garden. In these gardens, the pathways serve as unifiers, connecting one area to another for a different perspective. They also help to add a sense of wonderment and discovery. A pathway feature that encourages wandering satisfies the sense of curiosity. Gravel crunching underfoot or the calming sound made when walking on small pebbles becomes the music you hear as you move about. Pathways blend in with the landscape without becoming a distraction. Walking barefoot on smooth rocks has a relaxing effect, which helps to focus and become more aware of the natural setting.

Plants also set the tone in a Japanese style or Asian-themed garden. Usually, shades and textures are the common thread in these garden styles. The abundance of green—from chartreuse to emerald—creates a sense of calmness that is felt throughout the garden. Shrubs might have a seasonal bloom, however when the bloom is finished, green foliage remains as part of the backbone of the garden. Blooms or variegated foliage often complement in the garden (not contrast). Other plants are grown simply to tie together a concept within the garden. These plants are generally unobtrusive and do not distract from the serenity found within the garden.

Lastly, the architecture is simple. Common components are lanterns, a fence, a bridge, and a welcoming gate to name just a few. Lanterns might have a solar light or the option of using candles. There are string lanterns that can be draped from the tree limbs adding a certain peaceful ambiance to the area. Occasionally a gate or bridge might be painted red as a vivid accent. In today's Asian-themed gardens, decorative elements often have a shock of color. Any addition of colorful accents is at the discretion of the homeowner. Additional accents that do not distract from the serenity of the garden can reflect the whimsical spirit of an urban setting.

There are other elements found in Asian-themed gardens that are easily incorporated into the smaller urban garden. This theme can also be utilized on a balcony. Plants in pots, a lantern, and some form of water positioned in a corner, can easily create a garden with the theme of peace and serenity.

Cottage Garden

A colorful alternative in the urban garden is the cottage garden. Planting a cottage garden utilizes plants from many categories. Using annuals, perennials, and biennials, these gardens can boast season-long blooms. Cottage gardens are a great way to express the personality of the homeowner.

Cottage gardens have changed over time to reflect whatever trends are popular. A typical cottage garden contains five elements that are incorporated in the design. Some form of low fencing is woven into the garden. Usually, this fence separates the floral section of the garden from the vegetable section. Sometimes this fence merely serves as a support for a climber or a vine. The fence acts to elevate the plant, giving it a place where it can climb, drape, and roam. When used in cottage gardens today, these fences can also serve as colorful accents, serving to contain the garden and create garden rooms.

Cottage gardens usually offer some type of edible plantings. Traditional cottage gardens have included berry shrubs, herbs, and perhaps even edible flowers. It was common for the gardens to include something that was considered useful, edible and visually appealing. Today there are berry shrubs that can be grown in containers—a way to incorporate fruit in an urban garden. Perennial herbs and edible flowers, planted from seed, can also be potted up to add additional interest throughout the garden.

Fragrant flowers are commonly included in the cottage garden. Planted to coincide with the seasons, fragrant flowers allow the owner to glean bouquets for indoor use. Planting flowers with fragrance that evolves throughout the season adds interest to the cottage garden. Imagine walking by a colorful garden and a sweet scent wafts through the air. Planting various flowers that have fragrance as well as colors that pop is sure to catch the attention of passersby. Researching the sequence of bloom as well as the best fragrance time is key.

Tall plants and climbers can be found in most depictions of cottage gardens. Tall, sturdy, statement plants will allow the tendrils of annual vines to grasp and climb. Vines add a lot of depth to the garden. Growing horizontally or vertically, vines waft and weave without harming the existing plant material. This can create a tapestry not normally found in formal gardens. When a structure is added to the garden, blooming vines offer additional interest.

Using flowers that self-sow is an integral part of a cottage garden. The randomness of self-sowing plants adds a sense of comfort to the gardener from knowing that these self-sowers will always be seen throughout the garden. A cottage garden gives nature a way to sow beauty naturally. An added bonus of self-sowing plants is that they are almost never in the same place year after year.

Perennials that can be divided and moved throughout the garden are also a cost-saving option. This is one way the garden continues to reflect the personality of the owner. At the discretion of the gardener, seeds can be sown to try new plants or plants transplanted with a specific purpose in mind. Native plants can also be considered an integral part of a cottage garden. Native plants attract and provide food for pollinators. To some a cottage garden represents chaos. To others a cottage garden is a prime example of showing how well diversity works in the garden.

Creating a Collector's Garden

Many gardeners love collecting. From tools to books and even plants, we collect and sometimes hoard the things we love. The urban garden is the perfect place to showcase a particular collection of things that have has caught our eye. These are often considered collector or specialty gardens. Most urban gardens are limited in size which is perfect for creating a specialty garden. The collector or specialty gardener has often fallen in love with a specific plant or even type of art. Having a garden with collections of these favorite things can be quite beautiful.

One plant that offers subtle excitement to collectors is the miniature evergreen. These plants come in many colorful shades and interesting shapes. Miniature (sometimes they are called dwarf) evergreens can be grown in the ground or cultivated in a pot. They can be bred to grow very slowly or to maintain a moderate, but noticeable, rate of growth. Usually there is something of interest that makes them appealing to the collector—blue or silver needles, a compact shape, or golden foliage in the spring. Place the potted, collectible plants in an area where they cannot help but be noticed.

Having a dedicated area for the in-ground collection of plants is key. An area that is visible and easily accessible will ensure that these plants are well maintained. Adding subtle lighting is also a great way to showcase the intricate beauty of each plant. A mini spotlight can highlight or emphasize their special qualities. Consider adding small shelves to a fence to elevate rare species that might otherwise be lost in the landscape. Direct specialty solar lights on this area to add a touch of magic to their beauty.

Bonsai gardens can be truly intriguing. The bonsai collector usually has specific favorites that yearn to be the center of attention. This type of collector garden might only have bonsai in containers in various sizes. Using natural pedestals will add a special ambiance to the bonsai. Consider using stacked stones. Making sure they are steady, add a flat stone on top to accommodate the intended bonsai planter. Once in place, this will create an elegant focal point. If wood is your preference, consider using a unique piece of driftwood. Dig down into the soil to make certain the driftwood is level and stable. Add a flat piece of wood, stone, or even a piece of tempered glass as an elegant way to lift these bonsai specimens into a prominent position in the garden.

A garden room that offers dappled sunlight is perfect for the art collector. Smaller, intimate gardens offer areas that will provide a bit of space to enjoy a unique specialty plant or even showcase art pieces. Consider adding works from a specific artist for consistency. Collecting whimsical sculptures, perhaps made from steel drums, can also create a memorable experience in the garden.

Having a smaller space to appreciate whatever you collect is the perfect setting for a specialty or collector's garden.

Woodland Shade Garden

Large trees offer one of the best environments for shade gardens. Consider trees as the backdrop in a journey that simply gets better over time. When planning a shade garden, note how much lighting enters the space. Deep shade and dappled shade offer opportunities for discovering different types of plants, bulbs, and tubers.

Dappled shade is the perfect setting for planting understory trees and shrubs. Appropriately spacing these throughout the garden helps set the stage for a lush landscape. Sometimes these understory plants have blooms or scent. This adds seasonal value that is often overlooked. Using trees with colorful foliage can offer a season-long pop of color as a bonus. Usually, these small trees or large shrubs perform before the overhead tree canopies fully leaf out.

Leaving some leaf litter to decompose helps build nutrient-rich soil that generally stays moist throughout the season. Mimicking the forest floor is a terrific way to encourage native species of shade plants to thrive. Weeding out invasive plants and vines is easy due to the friable, rich soil created naturally.

Use foliage in shade gardens to make the ultimate statement. Just like in a natural woodland environment, some plants require minimal soil to thrive amidst the tree roots. Light, airy foliage rises and adds structural interest. Sometimes these plants spread and cover large areas on their own, such as ferns. There are even some plants that bloom and then have interesting foliage after the blooms. Several species of plants will self-seed naturally when nutrient-rich soil is present. Seedlings can crowd out weeds and create a bountiful amount of even more plants. Some perennials can produce a carpet of seedlings that can be transplanted when they are large enough. When the soil is moist and well balanced, plants usually tend to thrive on their own and multiply.

Adding blooming annuals brightens up the shady border. Spots of white or other bright colors can be accents in a sea of green, add a twist to variegated foliage, and add drama to bold foliage. Pots of annuals can be moved about in the shade garden to add emphasis where it is most needed. Potted annuals or garden art also serve as placeholders in any areas where there are no existing plants.

Broadleaved foliage adds bold impact to the shady border. In some plant cultivars, the foliage arises in ways that are quite noticeable. From variegated tips to odd-colored nubs, foliage arising in the shade border can add interest before the plant matures. Once the foliage opens up in the spring, there are often color changes, spires that signal future blooms, and late-season color. Collecting specialty plants or other interesting items to be included in the woodland garden offers unique experiences that will enhance the time that gardeners spend outside.

Tropical Jungle Garden

No matter where you live, a tropical landscape is easy to mimic in the garden. It can be fun creating a space where you feel that you are in a vacation-like setting right in your own yard. Start with something tall to mimic the overhead tree canopy. This canopy is a key element when planting a tropical-themed garden. Shade-producing overstory plants will keep this area cool when air temperatures are at a summer peak. Broadleaved plants can provide optimal coverage overhead when used to mimic the effects of dappled light.

When planning to build a tropical jungle garden, think about the site and what the existing plants need. The best place to create this new themed garden is in an area that gets sun but has plants that will withstand dappled light in the heat of summer. At the appropriate time, add the new first-tier plants. If they overlap, that is fine. Make certain that some light and rain can permeate the first-tier canopy, allowing the understory plants to benefit from a rainwater drink.

Medium-height plants can be the focal points of the tropical garden. Usually, these plants are at or slightly above eye level. Think about textural interest when choosing these second-tier plants. Loose, airy foliage will allow a breeze to circulate throughout the space. Grouping different types of layered, airy foliage can create a vignette that can be changed depending on plant lighting needs. If the plant combinations block air flow, changing them around will help. Consider adding multiple plants with different leaf types at intervals through-out the garden. Diversifying the space through the use of differing leaf shapes, colors, and densities will add visual interest that will create a tropical mood.

Utilizing common houseplants can add un-imagined interest when creating a tropical garden. These would be considered the third-tier plants. Indoor plants grown as parlor plants during the winter can help punctuate dark areas of the outdoor summer garden. The humidity and dappled light are exactly what is needed for them to thrive. In some instances, specialty houseplants often perk up when spending the summer outdoors. Mixing tropical plants and houseplants in with existing plant material will often create a unique palette that requires minimal maintenance.

Add plants that are low maintenance but contribute color. Annuals that bloom in shaded areas are the perfect way to add pops of color in unexpected areas. Leaf color can also set the tropical mood. Imagine using lighter color foliage to line pathways accompanied by large, lush, foliage-filled pots with or without blooms. This will create an instant tropical garden room in your own backyard. In areas where it might seem too dark, adding pots of colorful plants will liven up the area and capture your attention. Creating these colorful vignettes will allow the tropical-like foliage or blooms to become the focal point.

Tropical-themed gardens can often help as a transition to bring the inside living area outdoors. Creating a garden space that is easily transformed into a private tropical getaway can be created with ease if you use your imagination. Identifying the appropriate site and utilizing the existing landscape is the beginning of creating a lush tropical landscape right at home.

Meditation Garden

Having a place in the garden to settle our minds and sit quietly with our thoughts is important. Urban living can sometimes be filled with many unwanted distractions. A quiet space outside where we can meditate aids in calming the mind. Consider creating a meditation garden in a spot in your landscape that is out of the way. It might be a corner nook, behind a shrub border, or even tucked alongside the house. A place to meditate should be welcoming but be as private as possible. Consider ways that you can use this space and block exterior noises, which can be distracting.

Consider using shorter, grass-like plant material that could be considered as a sort of carpet. This is a great way to insulate the space from unnecessary noise. These low groundcovers can sometimes turn the area into a very desirable shoeless environment. Appropriate stepping stones or even a pebbled pathway will help create a sense of calm as you enter the designated area. Smooth stones underfoot are considered grounding influencers. The pressure points of relaxation within the soles of the feet can be activated when walking without shoes in the outdoors.

Medium-height shrubs and sometimes small trees can be used to create a living wall. These elements offer a mid-height softening of exterior noise as well as create a sound barrier. Muffling out exterior noise is an essential factor when creating a serene spot for meditating. When selecting trees or shrubs, consider an airy or layered effect. This will help creating an acoustical space, where sound blocking happens naturally at different levels. Depending on your climate, evergreen shrubs can extend the use of this space year-round, so it can be enjoyed in any season.

By using diversity in leaf texture, as well as height, this space can provide much enjoyment as well as a calming visual experience. The options are vast if you consider different shades of any soothing color. Layering and overlapping of this foliage will add unexpected points of interest. This can be achieved even if the palette is a calming shade of green with no additional spots of color. Add perennials that offer textured leaves. There are even some perennials or subshrubs that have insignificant blooms that will lend a calming effect. These blossoms do not distract from the ambience found within the space. Instead, they add a sense of balance and allow the eyes to rest. A pleasant scent is a welcome addition to most environments and the perfect way to add value to the meditative experience.

The art of meditation often includes some type of water feature. Water has been known to encourage relaxation. This can be achieved by incorporating a small water feature. A simple drip or the trickling sound of recirculating water can help with mindful focus. The rhythm of the sound of water is soothing. Water in a meditation space can also be still. Adding a vessel to hold or capture water can be used as a focal point. A space for meditation in the garden is not hard to create.

Sensory Garden

In an urban setting, a sensory garden can have many uses. Including a space where the five senses can be stimulated is a great way to become engaged with the garden. Sensory gardens have been around since the beginning of time. These gardens encourage the opportunity to touch, feel, observe, smell, and hear. Often sensory gardens are useful to soothe our minds as we concentrate on our senses to relax, reflect, and regroup. In the hectic world we live in, a sensory garden is a welcome feature in the urban landscape.

The most basic of sensory gardens offers flowers in many colors, shapes, and sizes. The diversity found in colorful gardens can excite the visual senses. Bright, larger blooms in colors contrasting with deeper, jewel-toned, smaller blooms, all create a stir visually. A sensory garden can have clusters of color even in the winter when most color is usually lacking. Consider using shrubs with colorful stems, variegated foliage, and foliage that changes colors seasonally.

Encourage natural music in the garden by inviting birds to enjoy the seeds and nectar found within. Add a vessel for water to further encourage passing birds and other wildlife to pause for a sip or a bath. Even a small fountain, where the water trickles over rocks, can gently break up the silence and soothe the mind. The sound of water is known to have a calming effect. Consider adding chimes to provide music powered by the wind. All chimes are different. Take time to listen to a few chimes before settling on one for your garden. Some produce sounds to soothe or settle the mind, while others might gently clap creating a rhythmic effect to awaken the mind. The sound of a wind chime should not be jarring or bold—just a nice subtle addition to the sensory garden.

Encourage the opportunity to touch materials in the garden. Different textures will provide a connectivity with the environment. Some leaves will evoke a sense of warmth and even encourage one to linger longer. Foliage that is soft to the touch can be quite soothing when visitors are gently brushing by in the garden. Utilizing plants with fuzzy, ruffled leaves that spill into the pathways will encourage touch along the way. These leaves are sometimes hairy, making them a pleasure to rub and hold. A rough leaf might graze the skin and urge one to move through the garden faster. Consider plantings that will connect with people and place them where visitors can reach out and touch them while enjoying the garden. Moss-covered rocks and pathways encourage touching—feeling the moist, cool moss is calming.

Consider growing scented plants. A grouping of roses with a heady scent can be a pleasant surprise when entering a garden room. Also consider incorporating plants with scented leaves. When bruising the foliage, the scent lingers on the fingertips and often is released into the air. Spacing these plants throughout the garden will encourage guests to pause for a smell and savor the many different areas of the garden slowly.

Make certain to include things to taste while enjoying the sensory garden. It is as easy as picking a leaf from a potted mint plant, plucking a tomato from the vine, or even using a few herbal leaves steeped in a pitcher for tea. Use other edible flowers that can be incorporated into salads or used for cooking. A small kitchen garden will provide the diversity needed to encourage lots of tastings as things ripen.

Adding a few of these sensory essentials in an urban garden setting will encourage frequent use and enhance enjoyment of any outdoor space.

Knot Garden

Knot gardens add a touch of formality and incorporate an organized feel in the urban garden. Knot gardens were initially designed to look like a knotted rope, only using plants. Specific border plants were used to create square beds with plants interwoven in a geometric pattern within the squares. These gardens were originally designed to be viewed from indoors, above the garden. The knot garden was usually the center of attention in the garden and known to be quite the visual statement. Today's knot garden can be an eclectic mix of formal and whimsy in its design. In an urban setting, the rules are a bit more relaxed.

Placing a knot garden in an easily accessible place is key. Access to all sides is critical for maintenance because the border plants that define the outline will need frequent trimming. This will require frequent visits. Selecting the appropriate plant material for a clipped hedge effect is important. Originally, aromatic herbs were used to outline knot gardens. Today, knot gardens are often comprised of an evergreen outline using plants such as boxwood or germander. Low- to medium-height evergreen shrubs or herbs that are easily sheared to a specific height, are frequently chosen.

Once the desired perimeter pattern is selected for each square, deciding what to include in the middle of the knot garden is next for the homeowner. Simple colored stones, sand, or even pavers have been traditionally used for the interior area and offer easy maintenance. Herbs, annuals, and even perennials have also been used within the designated squares of a knot garden.

Providing seasonal interest in the knot garden is easily achieved if planned properly. Consider adding bulbs to the middle of each section that, when flowering, will rise above the neatly clipped hedge plants. A planting of tulips amid an evergreen hedge outline really makes a striking statement. Centering these bulbs in the very middle allows other plants to fill in around them and provide seasonal color later.

Alternatively, sowing seeds for a mini meadow that will grow on top of a bulb planting in each defined square area can add informality to the knot garden and ever evolving interest. The meadow seedlings will grow and cover the browning foliage of the tulips or other bulbs. Depending on the meadow seed mix, the meadow can be filled with self-sowing annuals or perennials with varying bloom times.

In milder areas, some urban gardens use the refined formal appearance of the knot garden for winter interest only. During the warmer months, adding cold-hardy vegetables or even cut flowers gives a twist to the formal outline. Each section of the knot garden can be planted with one variety of crop or intermixed for an eclectic feel.

When deciding on a simple knot garden walkway, consider using sand or small pebbles in lieu of plant material. This will allow for the clean lines of the knot garden to stand out even more. Perhaps an art piece or fountain will provide a statement for the very middle, allowing the knot garden to become a three-dimensional centerpiece in the garden.

In an urban setting, a knot garden can be formal or informal depending on the type of hedging and the plantings inside each square.

Potager Garden

An artfully designed garden filled with edibles is commonly known as a *potager*. These kitchen gardens can be as eclectic as the homeowner, however there are certain factors that should be implemented. The finished potager should be inviting as well as functional. The ability to use a potager all year-round adds value to the landscape, as well as encourages the homeowner to make use of it as often as possible.

Designing a potager is the initial step. Creating a traditional layout is not always required. In today's potager, a simple design will work best. Complementing the surrounding area and choosing the appropriate pattern will encourage the homeowner to engage with the garden as it evolves throughout the season. Geometric shapes were standard practice in designing potagers at one time. Designing your garden allows you the freedom to make it a formal garden or not. The kitchen garden beds can be rectangles, squares, or freeform shapes that repeat in a unique design. Make sure the design aesthetically works within the rest of the urban landscape. Defining the bed edges with a noticeable border plant further refines the space. Wall germander (*Teucrium chamaedrys*), lamb's ears (*Stachys byzantina*), dwarf boxwood (*Buxus cvs.*), or even nasturtiums (*Tropaeolum majus*) are just a few of the plants often used to make potager borders.

Consider where the vertical accents will be inserted. Vertical interests can change yearly or stay put and become stationary parts of the garden. A tree or shrub wall can serve as a vertical interest that is somewhat permanent. Tall annual crops like corn or a stand of pole beans can also be used to add vertical interest. Often fruit trees are dotted along potager paths as well as throughout the garden. These trees add additional shape, height, and, of course, fruit to be enjoyed each growing season.

Think about what colors will pop throughout the potager. When growing perennials in the potager, homeowners will know where the gaps are. Perennial herbs like lavender, chives, and tansy offer returning foliage and flowers, year after year. Repetition of these plants throughout the garden gives a sense of order to the space. Most potagers are abundantly filled to the brim and rarely have any gaps. Depending on your climate, self-sowing annuals such as alyssum, basil, parsley, and phacelia are excellent options that can be depended upon to pop up the next year throughout the garden. These self-sowing annuals serve as companion plants for the perennials and vegetables. Companion plants can increase the yield within the potager and are often used in floral bouquets, dried arrangements, or wreaths.

All potagers have a focal point. Consider using an arch, pillar, or a trellis to draw the eye into the garden. Any of these can be enhanced by growing a colorful, ornamental vine, pole beans, or even a climbing rose at the chosen focal point. Some potagers have a fountain or a statue as the center of attention. All pathways should lead toward and connect to the center of the garden. Using gravel, stones, shredded bark, or crushed oyster shells help give definition (as well as neatness) to the garden.

As the potager vegetables grow and are harvested for use, make certain that some fast-growing plants are available to fill in any voids. Marigolds or bush bean seeds are great to have on hand just for this purpose. As you enjoy the potager, remember to rotate the plants from time to time to avoid soilborne diseases.

Installing an Herb Spiral

Creating an herb spiral is a terrific way to add a creative twist to the urban garden instead of building a traditional formal herb garden. Herb spirals are a wonderful way to utilize space in the garden in lieu of pots. Including an herb spiral in the garden is a great way to handle the differing cultural needs of herb plants.

Herb spirals will typically need full sun. When the site has been selected, make certain that you are able to move around or reach the inner area of the spiral from each side to harvest your herbs.

You will need some plain cardboard and weed-blocking fabric or gravel to start this project. Avoid cardboard with leftover tape on it or that is excessively printed with ink. You will also need a hammer or mallet, tall stake, a medium-sized stake, and enough string to define the optimal size of your spiral.

The average herb spiral measures 6 feet (1.8 m) in diameter. The size of your space will determine if that is too big. If this is the case, consider installing a smaller version. While limited in space, a 3-foot (1 m) herb spiral will work just as well. This type of project can be installed within a raised planting bed or on a gentle slope. Ample rocks, bricks, or other creative materials will be required to fill in the tiers of the spiral. Good soil, compost, plants, and mulch will be needed to finish off the herb spiral. Here are the instructions to build your herb spiral.

1. Lay the cardboard or alternative weed-blocking material down to stop any unwanted plants from growing up into the spiral.

2. Hammer the taller stake into the center of the spiral site. Tie the string onto the ends of both stakes and use this to mark out the desired width of the spiral. The spiral does not have to be a circle. An oval or even an irregular shape can express the creativity of the homeowner. Some herb spirals incorporate a water feature or even a rain garden on the final layer.

3. Begin using the bricks, stones, blocks, or other materials to start building the spiral. As you begin to build up, allow a minimum of 12 inches (30 cm) in width for each tier for adequate planting space. If you are using a dry stacking method, use smaller stones or overlap the materials to minimize any gaps. Continue to curve inward as you spiral up to the center.

4. Mix the raised bed planting soil and any other desired amendments together on a tarp or in an accessible area nearby. Add this soil mix as you increase the height of the spiral. Feel free to add sticks, leaves, or other garden debris to the tiers under the planting mix. These ingredients will take up space at the base of each tier. As they break down and settle, they will also add nutrients over time.

5. Make certain the base is high enough to hold a minimum of 6 to 8 inches (15 to 20 cm) of soil.

Once the herb spiral is constructed, add the herb plants, water, and mulch. If there are obvious gaps in the sides of the herb spiral, add plants such as common thyme (*Thymus vulgaris*) or other creeping herbs. The possibilities are endless when incorporating an herbal spiral in the urban garden.

Medicinal Herb Garden

Growing a medicinal herb garden is a great way to have healing herbs at your fingertips. Medicinal herbs have been essentials in the garden for over sixty thousand years. Depending on the homeowner's space, taste, and needs, medicinal herb gardens can be included in the landscape whether grown in pots or in the ground.

Most medicinal herbs need full sun and many will thrive in lean soils with average moisture. These herbs can be harvested for use in tinctures, elixirs, tonics, and more. The easiest way to use certain commonly grown medicinal herbs is by creating tea blends. Beyond teas, the leaves of these herbs can be used fresh or even dried for later use.

Placement of the medicinal herb garden is important. Keep plants within reach in a designated pot, in a garden space close to the house, or nearby on a deck. Some herbs grow abundantly and will need to be harvested regularly. Depending on the herb, the blossoms, stems, and leaves can be used for homegrown medicinal uses. Make certain that the medicinal herb garden is not close to an area where pesticides or other chemicals are used.

One common plant found in a medicinal herb garden is stinging nettle (*Urtica dioica*). This plant is often found growing in meadows. As the common name says, it often stings when touched on the leaves and stem. This beneficial plant is high in nutrients. Most parts of this plant can be either eaten, ingested, or used in the garden. Once cooked, the stinging chemicals are removed from the plant. This plant can also be used as a soil amendment. Incorporating the stems, leaves, and finished blooms into the soil to make a great green manure. Turning the remnants of this plant and many other herbs back into the soil enhances the soil naturally.

Plantain (*Plantago major*) is another plant that is commonly found already growing in the landscape. Many homeowners try to remove plantain from their lawns and in the garden. Incorporating this herb into a medicinal garden can be quite useful—when you least expect it.

There are many other herbs with healing properties that can also be grown in a medicinal garden. There are even plants that can be used in a potted medicinal garden. A large planter can offer enough space for a combination of plants that can be considered your pharmacy pot. Useful herbs like garlic (*Allium sativum*), fennel (*Foeniculum vulgare*), and even lavender (*Lavandula angustifolia*) can be combined in a large planter and harvested for later use. Harvest the garlic early in the season and dry it for cooking. The lavender flowers can be used for sachets, poultices, and in cooking as well. Fennel is a beautiful plant that has anti-inflammatory and antioxidant properties and attracts many pollinating insects. The bulb, foliage, and seeds are used in cooking. Harvesting the seeds at the end of the season will also help deter an overabundance of this herb self-seeding in the garden.

It is important to research the herbs that will do well in your climate and soil conditions. Decide which herbs will be useful to have on hand for life's little emergencies and grow them within reach.

CHAPTER 7

Privacy Boosters

FINDING SOLITUDE IS often difficult for gardeners in urban areas. Neighbors surround us on all sides and sometimes above and below us too. Much as we all love living a stimulating existence, we need to be able to tune out and take a break periodically. Carving out a peaceful space is a primary necessity of modern life. Gardens have long provided that place of sanctuary and solitude.

The unique problems of making an urban garden space feel protected and cozy are addressed by the topics of this chapter. We outline smart fixes not only for strangers peering in, but also for other ways that the world intrudes in our personal spaces such as from sound pollution and glaringly bright lights.

Many of these privacy boosters include using plant groups for a specific effect and taking advantage of their unique attributes. Your region's plant choices may differ; however, you will be able to apply the same principles using those plants locally available to you.

Creating a Shady Retreat

Shade is often overlooked when we consider building beautiful gardens. Creating elements in the garden to provide shade is easier than one might imagine.

Finding respite from the sun on a warm day is often difficult. Instead of looking for a large tree, create your own garden shade. Consider adding a few small trees for dappled shade instead of one large tree. Include these small trees along the perimeter of the garden or as a focal point within the garden. Allow room under the trees for a small bench, chair, and side table to use while resting and drinking water. If the setting is inviting, you might want to linger under this tree canopy even when it is not hot outside.

Arbors and pergolas also offer options for creating a shady nook. Positioned in full or part sun, they offer many possibilities for growing different kinds of plants that will climb up and over them. Arbors are usually sturdy enough to provide stability for a moderate-growing vine, such as clematis. These vines love cool feet, which makes the sides of an arbor perfect for them to grow up. Adding a seat directly under the arbor provides a place to pause and enjoy the view, even if there is nothing in bloom at the time. Adding lattice to the arbor provides a framework or backdrop for plants of all types. Consider dressing up the arbor with creative planting pockets or weave fabric through it as an accent. Plant a vine at the base of either side and weave it through as you train the vine to grow up. This will create a pleasing and shady place to pause.

A pergola can really make a statement in an urban garden. One with strong, sturdy beams will allow the creative homeowner to think outside the box. Adding roll-up bamboo screening to the top will create a cozy, covered shady room below. This creates the perfect outdoor living room. Accessorize to taste and you have made a sun-filled space into a shady retreat.

Adding shade on demand allows the homeowner to experiment with using tents. Tents can add a sense of whimsical adventure to any space. Pop up tents can be accessorized with lights for night or misting fans to cool during the day.

Children love adventure. If you have young children and want them to be outside on a hot day, consider using a tent. This adds fun and intrigue to a space of their own and is perfect for napping. Tents can be decorated inside as well as outside to embrace an adventurous theme just for children. They are also portable, allowing them to be placed on any level surface.

Fabric sails are perfect for small gatherings or can simply be erected over a lounge chair so the homeowner can sit with a book and read the afternoon away. Using one (or three) can create a colorful place to pause when the sun is just too bright. These are commonly adjustable and have three legs with stakes at the end. Sink the stakes into the garden or anchor the legs with sandbags. Provide seating or large pillows and you are ready for anyone to take a break. Creating shade in the urban garden is easy if you simply use your imagination.

Structures for Screening

Structures in the garden have many purposes. You will need to decide on the purpose, the type of materials used, and how sturdy the structure has to be. A simple frame is always a great starting point. These can be made of treated wood or some type of composite material that will resist rotting from exposure to the elements.

Make certain the structure is appropriate to the scale of the site. Allow room to move around it, as well as to walk within the structure, if it is not attached to an existing building such as the house. Anchor all structural posts in concrete or a similar substance to keep them firmly in the ground. Measure and use the appropriate in-ground support to ensure the structures are level.

One easy-to-use material for screening is lattice. Lightweight, easily secured, and inexpensively replaced, lattice is a great starter material to use in the urban garden. A simple lattice screen, secured as much as possible, can be enjoyed for years. Of course, there are more artistic options. Creative laser-cut screens are a great way to include art in the garden and have the use of a screen. These decorative screens should be secured in the middle, as well as on the ends, for stability. Often made of a composite material, these artfully curated screens last for quite a while. If you decide to replace the background, this is quite an easy task. Consider using all weather screws when installing these panels for ease of replacement.

Why stop at hard panels? Adding fabric to complement the garden is always an option. Choose loosely woven prints or solids to add a sense of drama to the garden. If stationary, make certain they are anchored into the ground properly. A dowel or curtain rod can be secured inside the frame at the top and the bottom to securely hang colorful fabrics. Adding fabric to a simple frame or having a few fabric panels strategically placed in certain areas of the garden, creates an intimate setting. Consider using fabric panels to create a private outdoor space for uninterrupted studying or even to take a well-deserved nap.

Fencing can also become a creative way to screen out unwanted views. There are many options other than the traditional 6-foot (1.8 m) wooden panel. Consider a shorter picket or artistically designed metal fence. Add a non-traditional panel above the traditional wooden panel to add a unique flair. Framed properly, these panels could also be painted and become garden art. Perhaps the structure could tell a seasonal story. Imagine seeing your favorite flower painted on a fence panel when winter is in full swing. This will bring a smile on any day.

Using branches, vines, or twine to create a wattle fence is a unique way to naturally add a touch of privacy. The diversity of the woven branches will add depth and texture. Lay the first row of branches and vines horizontally on the ground. Place the upright supports. The spacing of the upright supports should be considered so that it is even for the length of the wattle fence. One by one, lay more branches horizontally on top of the first layer, weaving them through the upright supports. Decide which edge will be the bottom and make sure it is even. Weave supple vines or twine under and over the branches if you don't use upright supports. Occasionally push the branches together to ensure they are tight. Adding natural elements intermittently such as twig balls or large seed heads adds unexpected interest as well. For another twist, consider leaving a gap to include a planted moss pocket that will thrive on the shady side of the wattle fence. Fencing does not have to be boring or traditional.

Fabric Screening and Décor

Creating a space that reflects the personality of the owner can be fun. Using an area to provide outdoor privacy can be as unique as the owner. Decorating this space with fabric also adds drama. Treat this space as an outdoor extension of the living room.

If you have a covered terrace or deck, add rods or clips inside the overhang to display your favorite treasures. Decide if you want to add additional fabric to allow for drop-down screening on one or more sides. A neutral or light, semi-sheer fabric works best and will allow the wind to flow generously. If the fabric of choice is too heavy, airflow will be minimal, and the fabric weight can strain the structure. Make certain the structure can handle lightweight but sturdy fabric when it is wet. The fabric can be secured at the top with a curtain rod or clips. A corner post with tie-back hooks can be used for anchoring and keeping fabrics secure. Longer lengths of fabric can also be allowed to drape and puddle onto the deck or ground within the garden.

There are creative options to consider when you are lacking corner posts. Think about adding a sturdy post cemented into a pot and positioned in place. Only fill the pot one-third full with cement. Once firmly in place, use the space around the posts to install colorful potted plants that can be changed throughout the season. Adding other creative elements like colorful stones, glass balls, or other unexpected seasonal accents keeps the garden uniquely fun. Add brackets for tying the fabric back at intervals.

Another option is to add simple drawstring ties strategically attached on the edge of an overhanging canopy. Sheer fabric, gathered and tied will create a simple barrier. If too much sun comes in on one side, releasing the tie and letting the fabric fall in place gives addition protection from the sun's rays.

Keep your color scheme in mind. Once the foundation color is in place, choose fabrics for additional accent pieces. Choosing fabric for floor coverings (as well as screening) is one way to begin building a color theme. Oiled canvas rugs can be utilized as an easy-care floor or ground covering. Usually found in bright colors, these add a pop of excitement to a private space.

Large floor pillows offer options of additional seating for lounging or entertaining. These pillows should be soil- and water-resistant enabling them to tolerate the elements. A cluster of three or five is usually enough to accommodate unexpected company. Consider a mix of designs or coordinated prints. In most instances, matching is not required. Coordinating fabrics with assorted prints or patterns allow the style or color of the chairs to help keep the theme intact.

Adding colorful vases, placing art on the walls, and carefully selecting books help create the perfect outdoor setting. Step back and see if there are any gaps where a pop of color is needed. If needed, add large pots of plants that echo or draw out specific colors. Using fabric to create a festive outdoor living room can bring out the creativity of the homeowner.

Vines for Privacy

Privacy in urban communities is often quite challenging. Renovated houses are often in older communities where every inch counts. Creating cozy, private spaces through the creative use of vines is one solution. Use this creativity to your best advantage by choosing the proper vine.

There are annual vines, which can be started indoors during the winter months. Some annual vines can also be directly sown in the ground outdoors at the appropriate time. When choosing annual vines, the homeowner can decide which seasonal color blends best with the garden, as well as the timing of the blooms. There are vines that bloom in the morning and some that only bloom at night. These vines can attract insects that can be quite beautiful as well as beneficial.

Perennial vines offer a different mindset. These vines will return year after year and become quite robust over time. These vines will need to be pruned yearly, as well as trained over a strong structure like a trellis, fence, or arbor. When training these vines, the homeowner should consider the maintenance required. Some delicate perennial vines have specific pruning requirements. Improper pruning can remove potential blooms. There are times when the vines may have to be pruned for stronger

growth. A weak vine can invite disease and pests, resulting in a less-than-perfect privacy screen.

Knowing whether a perennial vine is invasive is important. If an invasive vine is selected, make certain all shoots are contained and do not escape to grow on an unintended surface. A good gardener makes certain that all berries or blooms are cleaned up in order to prevent unwanted seedlings. A good privacy vine is one that is controlled by the owner.

There are some vines that offer privacy even when there is no foliage. The structure of their branching offers a semi-transparent screen. These vines can be trained throughout the growing season. They have supple, easy-to-weave branches that are often braided or twisted to form a trunk. Once created, the trunk is a work of art. Weaving the new growth will help increase the density of the living privacy screening. This is helpful when entertaining during the off-season. While not totally a wall, this type of see-through screen is merely a good buffer.

In some areas there are evergreen vines. These vines are commonly used as living privacy screens when dwellings are simply too close. These vines are generally easy to maintain and long-lived. Pruning these evergreen vines to fit a specific structure is an art form. Tucking in new growth and regularly pruning them so the vines stay relatively dense is key. Observe them closely to avoid disease or pest damage.

Proper maintenance of privacy vines to ensure healthy growth for optimum coverage of any structure is important. Make certain air circulation is provided and that the structure is compatible for the vine. A heavy vine needs a heavy-duty structure. Deciding on how much privacy you will need and when you need it is important when selecting a vine to act as a screen.

She Sheds and He Sheds

Sheds are quite useful in the landscape. Having a space to put stuff, pot plants, or just be, is important. Although often named she sheds, they can sometimes be considered he sheds too. No matter which gender they are called, whoever installs these little extensions of storage space, makes it personal. The function of each shed can be very versatile and reflect the personality of the owner.

Some of these sheds merely serve as a formal place to store tools and other garden accessories. Very organized, these spaces often have shelving, hooks, and include cubby holes for proper placement of hand tools. Bookshelves are often included, so the ability to search for plant information is merely a fingertip away. A stool for perching while transplanting seedlings or potting up planters also comes in handy.

Sheds can also be transformed so they become outdoor living quarters. Some sheds include all the creature comforts of a family room. Love seats, refrigerators, and even cooktops can be found in them. These types of she sheds are used primarily for entertaining. No need to entertain in the house when you have an outdoor living room. The rain or snow will not affect the opportunity to be in the garden with these buildings. Having a space for this purpose is an extension of the home, just in the garden. If an unexpected storm is on the horizon, a she shed allows the entertaining to continue without having to bring the guests inside the traditional home.

A shed can also be used as a studio or office. Built-in bookshelves allow the owners to have their favorite novels or even books in the "yet to be read" pile always available. Installing cable to the shed expands the opportunity to connect to the outside world via streaming shows, watching old movies, or even listening to music. As a workspace, a shed can be turned into a home office—drastically shortening the normal commute to the office. Even when not actually working from home, a shed can provide an alternative, multifunctioning space that is the perfect setting to be *at* home, but also *away* from home.

Imagine a place that is always there to escape from the woes of the world, consider a shed as an on-site getaway. Another useful way to use this space is as a yoga retreat or a meditation room. Create seating for pausing and relaxing, including having a mat for stretching, or even an oversized cushion for napping— all this makes it a space that celebrates calm.

When creating a she shed (or a he shed) you might include a mini refrigerator, a small TV, or simply have a radio. Many times, a shed can become a craft area. Woodworking might take place in this space so the noise and dust is not in the house. Having the ability to leave unfinished projects in place where you can resume them exactly where you left off (and everything is still there), is a gift.

Adding bountiful window boxes or even planting nearby gardens that include herbs for making tea, make these shed spaces an extension of whoever owns them. These sheds can be an asset when defining a space to call your own.

Water Features to Disguise Sound Pollution

The soothing trickle of water on stone is one of the most relaxing sounds in nature. A bubbling brook or gentle waterfall is a classic landscape element that can calm your nerves and immediately relax your mind. The movement of fresh, running water adds sparkle and life to any space.

A well-placed water feature in a small-space garden can disguise the noise of nearby traffic and passersby. They can also be used to mask unwanted sounds such as barking dogs or loud neighbors. This is the ultimate "white noise" machine.

The rate at which the water moves and the amount that circulates through the system can usually be adjusted on the pump. You can also purchase pond pumps with different flow outputs. The greater the flow, listed as gallons or liters per hour, the more splashing and water noise will be created.

Another way to increase the water splashing sound in a pond is by placing stones where they will be hit by the cascading water—creating more ambient noise. Placing a solid wall behind the feature can further amplify the water sound.

Water features for urban gardens come in many forms and sizes from tabletop bowls to small ponds. They can be filled with aquatic plants and be a home for koi or goldfish. Water gardens are very low maintenance and they don't need watering or regular weeding!

If you install a recirculating water feature, this will serve both as a lovely design element and provide clean water for the creatures visiting your garden. (See Nesting Sites and Water on page 188.) Constantly moving water also prevents mosquitoes from laying their eggs on the water surface.

To add extra privacy to your small garden, water features can be mounted on a wall or on a stack of small boulders. Pre-formed waterfalls or tall, cast concrete stones are available that are lightweight and can be used to add height to your water garden design.

There are also stand-alone recirculation water features that have a catchment system that is buried below the ground. These systems have pumps inside the structure that force the water up and over the sides of a large rock or container. You can buy this as a kit or create one yourself using an old, tall urn.

A small tabletop fountain in a bowl can also provide the tranquil sounds of running water and be tucked into any spot with a nearby power source. There are even fountain kits available with solar-operated panels, freeing you up from location restrictions.

Bamboo and Grasses in Containers

Your garden can be your sanctuary, but sometimes it can feel like everyone in your neighborhood can see into your private spot and you just want to have some alone time in your garden to collect your thoughts and experience some inner peace.

Garden screens and fences can be expensive and cumbersome. They can also take away valuable growing space or worse, they can block the sunshine that your plants need to grow. Such permanent barriers may also not be permitted by your landlord, community regulations, or building rules.

Tall grasses or bamboo planted in containers are the perfect solution for creating versatile privacy screens in small-space gardens. The plants can be placed in modular containers or pots with wheels, so that they can be moved around to create a quick screen or wall and then they can be placed off to the side when you are not in the garden so you allow in unobstructed sunlight.

Grasses and bamboos also add a bonus sensory benefit as they create a lovely motion and sound in the slightest of breezes. Their graceful movements are a pleasant cover for street noise, and they can also serve to partially block an unpleasant view. Swaying plants add another layer of charm to any garden.

There are hundreds of varieties of tall grasses and bamboos available. (Bamboo is actually a woody grass.) Choose one that will not grow too large for the container and space. Look for cultivars that are specifically bred for container use. Also seek out those that are cold hardy in your area as container plants are more susceptible to freezing temperatures.

Grasses and bamboos are very low maintenance. Just give them a dose of slow-release, high-nitrogen fertilizer once a year (according to the package instructions). They also require occasional pruning of broken stems and an annual cut-back of any winter-damaged foliage, if you live in a cold climate.

Container-grown grasses and bamboos also need more water than those grown in the ground, so check their moisture needs every few days. Bamboos, in particular, hate to dry out. In general, they require 1 inch (2.5 cm) of rain per week or they will need supplemental watering.

Container-grown grasses and bamboos grow more slowly than those planted in the ground, so you will need to plant them closer together than the plant tag recommends to create a fuller, denser look. For instance, if the tag says one plant per every 6 feet (1.8 m), you will instead plant one about every 3 to 4 feet (90 to 120 cm) apart. And when growing these in containers, you will have to remove and divide the plants every 2 to 5 years to prevent them from becoming root-bound.

Note that tall plants, particularly those in tall pots, can be easily knocked over by high winds. If your garden is in an elevated area, such as a balcony or rooftop, then strong winds are especially likely to impact your plantings. If that is the case with your garden, you might consider some methods for anchoring your containers in place. These could include chains that hook them to a nearby railing or placing a stake in the back of the pot and tying that stake to a permanent structure.

Pots are less likely to fall over if they are placed in groupings or in a corner. An attractive way to add weight to pots is to fill around the plant stems with river rock or pea gravel. You can also place a brick or large stone at the bottom of the planter before you fill it with soil. Of course, you want to make sure there are still plenty of holes open in the bottom of the pot to allow for the water to drain freely.

Living Walls and Hedges

Walls can often keep our neighbors as our friends. Living walls are a great way to suppress noise and block unwanted views without having the structure of a fence. Consider the options of using vines, a hedgerow, ornamental grasses, or a collection of evergreens as a living wall. The urban garden is usually a finite space. Too much wall volume will minimize the usable area, so the right selection is very important.

Vines are easy to grow. Whether they bloom or not, training vines to cover a fence for privacy will require a bit of work. Pruning shoots to maintain optimum coverage and density as the vine grows is important. Tucking in the occasional wayward shoot will keep the vine from overtaking other plants or structures. Weekly observation of your vines during the growing season can minimize the drastic measures needed as the vines mature.

Hedges can provide the needed privacy coverage when they are used as a living wall. Consideration needs to be given to the optimum height, lighting conditions, spread, spacing, and maintenance. Determining the optimum maximum height is important when selecting a hedge. Make sure you choose a hedge with growth expectations close to the height you desire. Pruning is essential to control the height of a fast-growing shrub. Also, consider the mature width of the hedge. You will need to plant the hedge plants far enough away from the property line to allow maintenance from all sides without stepping on your neighbor's property. Make certain of the lighting requirements for healthy hedge growth. Some shrubs will perform better with a buffer to protect them from the strong sun. Other shrubs can struggle and become bare in spots due to the lack of enough sunlight. Decide if you want fast hedge coverage or if you are satisfied with a slow-growing, minimal-maintenance shrub. Does the hedge have to be evergreen? Many deciduous shrubs will bloom during the summer months but are bare in the winter.

Ornamental grasses should also be considered as an option for a living wall. Offering a diverse range of foliage, color, height, and width, grasses can be chosen to suit a variety of conditions. When swaying in the wind, ornamental grasses also provide movement in the landscape. Some cultivars offer late-season color or plumes. Left standing during the winter months, ornamental grasses become architectural statements in the landscape.

There are certain evergreen combinations that also work well together as a screen. Look for foliage variations in color, as well as texture. Certain colors will play off each other at different times of the year. Foliage with yellow and blue undertones tend to stand out in the winter landscape. Evergreens with darker foliage form the perfect backdrop during the warmer months.

A living screen is something to embrace for quite a while. It should be appealing and something you can live with for many years. Carefully consider the purpose of any living wall. When selected and maintained properly, it is the perfect living privacy screen.

CHAPTER 8

Recycled & Repurposed Inspiration

WHETHER YOU ARE on a tight budget or are merely frugal by nature (as both of your authors are), upcycling items in the garden can save you time, effort, and money. In addition, reusing the limited resources available in your local area displays good stewardship of our shared environment and the planet.

There is a gravitas and provenance to repurposed items that newly bought ones don't have. Whether or not you know their back story, an antique or vintage tool feels different when using it and connects you to those previous gardeners and owners. Aged and weathered items used ornamentally also lend a layer of history and depth to a garden.

Read on for creative ways to recycle and reuse various items collected from nature, at secondhand shops, or from your own garden shed.

Containers Made from Discarded Antiques

If it can hold soil in it, it can be a planter. Keep that mantra in mind when visiting charity stores, secondhand sales, or just rummaging around your own attic. When scouting for possible containers, consider how the item might age and weather outside. Wooden crates and woven baskets last a few seasons, while metal, ceramics, and plastic often endure for many years.

Kitchen and bathroom fixtures withstand the outdoors quite well and still have decades of life left in them. For instance, big, old, clawfoot tubs make wonderful raised beds. Sinks can support a variety of succulents and the empty burners of kitchen stoves are a perfect fit for small planting pots.

Old beds can become a fun element in the garden too. Ideas include literally framing a garden bed with an old brass headboard at one end or standing a bed spring up against a wall and weaving vines through it or clipping little planting pots onto it.

Children's toys and clothing, such as metal trucks and worn-out rain boots, are another option for planters that will become a special conversation piece in the garden. Some toys can be modified by cutting out a section to grow plants in—like a plastic dinosaur or a doll's head.

Chairs of all sizes are a classic garden accessory. Cut a circle out of the seat bottom and plop in a container that fits snugly in it or simply place a plant pot on the chair seat itself.

As with all plant containers, drainage is key. If the vintage items you are using don't have enough holes weathered into them, you will need to drill in additional ones. A good guideline to follow is two or three holes per square foot of growing space. Err on the side of more drainage holes, rather than less here.

Don't forget that items may be placed on their sides or turned upside down. An old metal mailbox sat on its end makes a delightful planter. As this mailbox (shown here) is fairly deep, a false bottom is inserted about half-way up so the soil and plants are just in the upper half.

A collection of tea tins and biscuit boxes planted with herbs looks lovely sitting on a table or shelf in the garden. One note of caution here. Rusty patinas look beautiful in the garden, however, they can permanently stain your hardscape surfaces. To avoid getting rust rings on your pavers or decking, coat the bottom of any rusting antiques with a sealant spray. Also, wear thick gloves when handling them to avoid getting cut by any sharp metal edges.

Remade Tools

Never throw out an old hand tool. The handles may break, but there is still much life in them. Sometimes, these handles are easily replaceable. Other times, it might be difficult to find a matching handle, though you should still hang on to the metal portion of your hand tools, as you never know when a handle match or other use might be found for them. Keep a bucket handy for storing these tool pieces until a new purpose for them springs to mind.

There are many ways to remake old metal tools into new practical and decorative objects. Don't discard the broken handles either! They can still last for several more years as trellis supports, plant stakes, etc.

Rake heads are extremely versatile. Mounted on a bed or fence, they make terrific hanging racks for storage of all kinds of garden-related items—from drying herbs to hanging small tools. Similarly, the head from an old leaf rake serves well as a place to organize and dry your garden gloves or for displaying seed packets.

The ends of shovel handles make a fun door knocker or drawer pull. Shovel heads can be bent at the base and screwed onto a fence post to create a shelf surface to place bird seed or set out a small herb pot. A series of these along a walkway is quite charming. Insert a few old hand trowels or small hoe heads in the ground as hose guides or border edging.

Mount a rusty saw on a board and then paint it with your address numbers or with a cheery "welcome!" for the front entrance.

Open an old metal toolbox and add some soil, then plant it up with a collection of hardy sedum and cacti. Place metal wheelbarrows and children's wagons with broken axles or wheels on the ground to use as fire pits or planters.

If you are feeling creative, borrow a soldering iron and attach several old tools together to form a crow to watch over your garden or craft really any animal or shape that you desire as a decorative guardian.

Growing Vertically in Repurposed Rain Gutters

Have you ever walked by an abandoned home and seen trees growing out of the gutters? This is a testament to how well they work for holding soil and moisture.

Rain gutters come in various widths and materials. The least expensive types are aluminum, vinyl, or PVC. These are lightweight and easy to work with. You can cut them with tin snips or a hacksaw and drill through them quite easily. Look for the kinds with open tops. Also remember that you will need to put on end caps to hold in the potting soil. Spray paint the gutters for a whimsical effect or leave them in their original shiny metal or vinyl finish.

The length of the gutters is up to you. A series of 6-foot- (1.8 m-) long gutters hung horizontally on a fence a foot or two apart can quickly multiply your available growing space.

If you are renting your urban garden space, running gutters along your table edges or placing them in freestanding racks is a semi-permanent option. Hanging them on a system of connecting chains is another possibility.

Add drainage to the gutters by drilling holes every few inches. Cut a length of weed barrier fabric to line the bottom and hold in the soil. A light, soilless potting mix is best for this shallow container. Also, remember to mount the gutters on your wall or fence at a slight angle to help with drainage.

Because the gutters are fairly shallow, your plant choices are limited to those with short roots. Try lettuce and other salad greens, herbs, succulents, strawberry runners, and some annual flowers. These can be switched out seasonally. Keep in mind that the top gutter will obviously get the most sun and also get the most rain, so the bottom layers may need more supplemental watering.

Plants in shallow gutter planters require extra fertilization because the soil cannot hold onto many nutrients. You will also need to switch out the potting mix annually.

Recycled Bottles for Borders and Walls

Recycling materials used in the landscape offers many different options. Using glass bottles in the landscape can offer many opportunities to expand your creative boundaries. Your imagination is the key. Consider mingling glass bottles and inexpensive glass vases to create a wall.

Wine bottles, perfume bottles, and more are the perfect item to repurpose into wall art. When creating a glass bottle wall make certain the supporting beam or frame will adequately hold the weight of the recycled material. Strong cable or wire will be necessary to stabilize the bottles if they sway in the wind. Inserting a buffer of some type between the bottles will keep them safely in place. These buffers can be large, recycled beads, bottle tops, or even metal discs. The circumference of the buffer will need to be large enough to separate each bottle. Drill a hole in the bottom of each bottle (with the appropriate drill bit) to allow for individual threading of the bottles. Allow your creativity to take charge. Using glass containers of various colors, shapes, and sizes will make this

project fun. The fun is with the selection of each bottle, choosing its placement, and creating your work of art for the garden.

Mixing glass bottles with medium-sized stones can also unleash your creativity and make a dynamic wall. Take yourself on an artistic adventure by selecting stones that complement the color of the bottles used. A stable foundation of stone is important to hold up the wall over time. Cutting out the backs of the bottles with a glass cutter will help create a uniform depth to the wall. Depending on how thick the finished wall is, these little nooks can be used for beautiful found stones, mini bouquets, or even succulent plantings. As you build the bottle wall, inserting special accents will create a unique artistic display that is all your own. Balancing glass and stone can prove to be a challenge, but a fun and creative one.

Bottles as a border or a wall, can last a long time if you are cautious. Digging a 10- to 12-inch-(25- to 30-cm) deep trench to support the wall is essential. Some choose to insert the bottles straight down. Others choose to angle the bottles, which allows any water or snow to run off into the garden. Leaving the bottle bottoms exposed adds eclectic character to the garden. These bottle borders can be all the same height or built at uneven heights just for fun or to highlight a specific plant. Bottles can be used along walkways to provide definition (and a smile). By placing the bottles in the ground at or below the frost line, the homeowner can enjoy them for many years to come.

Using recycled glass bottles or vases is a creative way to define boundaries in the urban garden.

Mixing in Natural Decorative Elements

Despite being full of plants and furnishings, many city gardens appear sterile or devoid of life. What they are missing is a layer of organic materials that naturally occur in more rural gardens, but may not be as readily available in urban settings.

Cure this "sterile hotel room" effect by adding in natural items that build on the story of your garden and reflect your interests and personality. Display a fossil or a handful of sea glass on a shelf among your watering cans and other garden supplies. A twisty piece of driftwood forms a fine centerpiece on any outdoor table.

Any collection of natural elements gathered in a bowl or basket is attractive. Pinecones, shells, and stones all can be collected easily on your travels and then placed about the garden. Contain more delicate items like seed heads or dried flowers in a glass jar or large vase.

Really special items should be placed inside a terrarium, apothecary jar, or other enclosed glass space where they can be viewed, but not handled. These might include a shed snakeskin, an empty bird's egg, animal bones, or a turtle shell.

A line of buckets full of soil amendments will add a real earthiness to your garden. From sand to compost, these containers can be placed under a bench so the contents stay relatively dry. Paint on a label so you know which is which when you need to retrieve and use them.

Neatly stacked logs and bundled sticks are always pleasing to the eye and can be used in an outdoor fireplace or just gathered as a decorative element.

Going one step further, weaving willow sticks or bamboo together for fencing is an attractive way to cover up an ugly wall or view.

Hang some dried grapevine on a wall or fence that has been twisted into a loose wreath. Leave it plain and simple or insert some other natural items into it such as seedpods or cotton balls for decoration.

Found or purchased natural objects are the perfect way to level-up an urban garden.

Bringing Inside Décor Outside

Outdoor living is not a new trend. Since ancient times, people have brought the creature comforts from inside their homes out into their garden space. In a small garden especially, the lines between inside and outside can easily get blurred because you are treating the outside as an additional indoor room space.

Your first consideration when bringing inside décor items outside is whether or not they can withstand the natural elements. Consider exposure to wind, sun, cold, heat, wet, and also wildlife. If the item is only semi-durable, you will need to remember to bring it inside when it is too windy, cold, or wet to leave it out.

Look for items that are labeled as suitable for indoor and outdoor conditions. These can have weatherproof finishes or be made of materials that hold up under various weather conditions. Specialty outdoor fabrics are very durable these days. Not only are they waterproof, but they also resist bleaching from the sun and are tough enough to take an occasional poke from a garden trowel accidentally left in your back pocket.

Sometimes a finishing coat of varnish or shellac is all that is needed to lengthen the life of an item. Other items that you might consider "indoor only" can sometimes prove to be surprisingly strong. Most things made from rubber, plastic, wicker, glass, ceramic, stone, concrete, metal, and wood do just as well when used outdoors as they would indoors.

Many gardeners like to bring reading materials out to peruse them. Magazines and books will not stand up to the outdoors without protection, but you can place them in a container for protection like in a large cookie tin or old breadbox.

Candles are great for creating a mood in the garden. However, even the slightest breeze or moisture in the air can snuff them out. You can solve this by placing them inside glass lanterns or tall, clear vases to protect them while still enjoying their light.

A throw or light blanket is also nice to have outside to curl up with on a cool day. These can be rolled up and stored inside a stool or an ottoman with a lid that pops off to provide extra hidden storage.

Decorating with loose hanging fabric is another indoor luxury that can transition to the outside area in the form of weatherproof curtains or mosquito netting. This can create a bit of shade where needed or privacy from prying eyes.

Don't forget to bring some simply beautiful indoor touches out into the garden. Try a crystal chandelier hanging from a pergola or strings of beads and costume jewelry threaded in nearby tree branches.

Finally, a vase filled with flowers from your garden or purchased at a farm market can grace outdoor spots wherever a spot of cheer is needed.

Art in the Garden

The size of a garden should have no impact on whether it features art in it or not. As a matter of fact, smaller gardens can be the perfect setting for certain art pieces that are meant to be seen up close. Some art is even created to be interactive, and encouraging touching and handling is part of the experience.

Art placed in a garden should be fairly weather-proof. You can look for a protected spot or make an alcove to display a piece that may not be very weather-tolerant. A spray or painted coat of polyurethane or shellac might be needed to further ensure the art lasts a long time.

Occasionally, an art piece is meant to be affected by the elements and should show wear and changes from the weather. This could be the deliberate aging of copper or bronze to show the resulting patina or a rusting pattern on a metal sculpture.

Various pieces of art are meant to be seen in a grouping or set. These can be used to a nice effect as a repeated element in the garden. (See Joy in Repetition on page 169.) Others need to be placed as a focal point to be enjoyed on their own. (See Creating Vignettes and Focal Points on page 165.)

Garden art need not be expensive. You can create art for the garden yourself with simple materials. Try creating a mosaic tabletop or painting an inspirational message on a salvaged wood board.

A trip to a secondhand store or salvage yard can be eye-opening. Look for unusual items or ones that can be used in new ways. An old phone booth can be fitted with shelves and used to store colorful pots and small tools inside. A large wheel or hoop can be mounted on a fence or used lying down set flush into the middle of a pathway.

Anything that holds soil can be reused as a planter—from teapots to office supplies. A tool box, tacklebox, or small suitcase is a popular choice for the garden edge, planted with annual flowers that will spill out of it.

Metal and wooden chairs that are missing their seats can be transformed into planters. Old bird cages can be hung up and filled with ferns or succulents. Large glass serving pieces can be stacked up and secured together with waterproof marine glue to create interesting and sparkly sculptures.

Old children's toys are a great source of garden art pieces. Plant up a small fire engine or dump truck. Line up doll heads in a row along a fence line. Give Barbie and her friends an outdoor, jungle-themed disco!

If something is broken or incomplete, you can bury it or lay it on its end or side. Letting nearby plants spill over onto an item can also help add a layer of mystery and disguise the missing edge or parts.

Don't discard an item that is faded and lackluster. A worn piece can be made new again with a fresh coat of spray paint. Other ways to breathe life into vintage items are by reupholstering them, stripping layers of old paint off them, or just giving them a thorough cleaning.

You might have some treasures sitting in your own storage areas that can get a second lease on life when featured as a piece of funky garden art.

Bed Edging Options

Edging your garden beds keeps visitors from stepping on treasured plants and makes weeding easier. A nice bed edging can also create an attractive boundary line that adds to the overall design and charm of a small garden.

Garden bed edges can be made from any number of materials. You want an edge that is noticeable so it is not a trip-hazard, one that is pleasing to the eye, and one that doesn't detract from the rest of the garden.

Bed edging can be a source of whimsy and a chance to show off your personality in the garden. Examples of recycled elements used for edging include seashells, bowling balls, hubcaps, and wine bottles turned upside down. Many gardeners collect rocks during their travels and then add them to their garden edges a little at a time.

Salvage yards are also great places to find edging options. You can find old bricks or other building materials that you can use as edging. Sometimes a found object might speak to you and suggest a new use. Terra cotta roof tiles look as good laid end-to-end or overlapping on the ground as they do on a roof.

Cinder (cement) blocks are another option that you can pick up cheap from an industrial materials or reuse store. They can be used for low edging walls positioned with the openings on the top that can be planted with succulents.

If you have willow growing in your garden or can source some, you might try weaving a low "wattle" fence. (See Structures for Screening on page 122.) Similarly, bamboo can be cut and pounded into the soil while still green or lashed together to form a short barrier along a bed edge.

Edging can be outlined at the start of a project but need not be finished right away. Part of the fun in using repurposed materials for garden edging is that it can be collected a few pieces at a time and added to over the years.

You might start off with wooden boards placed down as bed edges and then remove the boards (or shorten them) as your newly found recycled edging materials are added in. Or you can dig a shallow trench as a bed edge and backfill it when you have pieces to set in place there.

Depending on your own personal tastes and garden style, you might like a pathway edge that is "messy" and allows nearby plants to spill over it or you may wish to maintain a formal, clean edge. If you are the sort that prefers clean edges, you will want to invest in a few tools to maintain that sharp line and perhaps upgrade your pathways to a higher quality surface area such as bricks or interlocking pavers. (See Paths and Walkways on page 170.)

Plants themselves can also be trained and used as bed edging. Good choices for this purpose include boxwood, germander, and short ornamental grasses.

CHAPTER 9

Small-Space Solutions

THIS IS THE HEART of our book and we bet this is where you will glean the most applicable ideas for your garden. "Small space" is relative, of course. You might have acres of land on which to garden or a tiny terrace and still think of each as a small space. Small spaces challenge us, but they are also inspiring. These little jewel box gardens can allow us to design a perfect environment that is just right for our needs.

Discover how to make your small space feel more expansive as well as ways to cleverly expand the space you have. If you are lucky enough to have a larger space, you can apply the basic design ideas outlined here to spaces of all sizes. The design ideas are based on sound spatial principles gleaned from interviewing both expert landscape designers and amateur gardening enthusiasts.

The storage tips and other clever solutions offered here were collected from touring hundreds of urban gardens—from rooftop terraces to postage-stamp front yards. The gardeners we encountered on our travels were all very generous with their time and wisdom. We hope you can use their collected knowledge detailed here to make your garden a special place.

Designing Small Spaces to Feel Big

No one likes feeling claustrophobic in a garden. You want your small-space garden to feel cozy and welcoming, not one that barely leaves you the clearance to turn around and enjoy the surroundings.

There are a few tricks you can use to fool the eye and make the garden layout seem bigger. An easy one to do is to place the seating area one step up on a raised deck. Also, lighter-colored paving materials will give the illusion of a more open space.

Obscure the outer edges of your garden with climbing vines or tall plants to blur the boundaries and make it appear that your space continues farther than it actually does.

If your space is long and narrow, set your planting beds and furnishings at an angle of 30 or 45 degrees. This angular design avoids the "hallway effect" and makes the layout much more dynamic.

If your space is wide and square, make it seem less "blocky" by running a deep planting border along the back side and place an oval or round seating area off to one side and then install a series of long raised beds on the other side.

Also, think about overall scale. Large items may potentially dwarf their surroundings, but you also do not want to use a series of undersized pots and accessories as they can actually make the place feel even smaller and more cramped. Instead, use mid-sized items, just fewer of them. For instance, place a grouping of three good-sized pots together—one slightly smaller in height and diameter than the next—with the largest to the back and shortest to the foreground. This effect gives depth and perspective to the grouping.

The same stepping-up plan should be followed for garden plantings—with the tallest plants at the back, then a middle layer, and the shorter, edging plants at the front of the border. This draws the visitor's eye over and through the planting bed to the back.

Coordinate the hard surfaces in your garden for a harmonious look. For instance, don't switch from brick path to gravel to stone—all in one area. Change materials only when indicating a transition in elevation or when entering a new garden room or area.

Other tactics for creating a space that feels bigger are covered under separate chapters in this book, including making your pathways generous and wide, borrowing a view, and including reflective surfaces in the garden. And additional techniques that we cover in this chapter will literally give you more space to work with, including clever storage tips for tools and water.

Smart Use of Lighting

Lighting a garden sets the mood and expands the number of hours you can enjoy the space. It also provides an additional safety function, literally lighting the pathway for your garden visitors to walk.

A quick, easy, and inexpensive way to start adding lighting to the garden is with a string of fairy or holiday lights suspended above a seating or dining area. You can also achieve a welcoming glow with a series of lanterns hung along a fence line or pathway. Another idea is to group tea lights on a mirrored tray set on a table so they can reflect their pleasing glow back into the garden space.

Place battery-operated candles (or real ones) in glass hurricane lamps to protect them from the rain and wind. Many new landscape lighting options are available that use solar panels or rechargeable batteries built right into them. This frees you up from running long cords or having to be near an electrical outlet.

One secret to great lighting in a small space is to get visitors to look up, not just down. Instantly the garden feels more expansive and open when they do this. If you have trees surrounding your space, hang some lights in their branches or you can suspend lights from tall poles placed in the ground.

Another tip is to use spotlights to highlight an architectural element or other feature at night. A wide flood light facing a wall will show off the shadows and shapes of plants against it. A pinpoint light placed under a sculpture or large-leaved tropical plant such as a banana tree makes for a very dramatic impact.

As with many aspects of small-space gardening, don't overdo it. As the adage says, a little goes a long way. With outdoor lighting, that is particularly true. The experience should be of revealing subtle shapes, textures, and layers—not of an airport runway.

Go out at night and play around with your lighting and its effects. Ensure that the lighting isn't facing into anyone's windows and that it is the lowest wattage possible to minimize outdoor light pollution.

Pushing the Boundaries

Green spaces in the city are precious and there are long wait lists for community gardens and apartments with outdoor access. Inventive gardeners know that it is always possible to find a place to plant a garden. It might mean you have to get creative and resourceful to find your own little Eden, but it is possible.

Ask around at work and among your friends and family to find out if someone has a part of their property that you can use for a garden, perhaps in exchange for a share of your flowers or produce.

Volunteer at a local school garden, park, or public gardens. Many of the organizations that run these places offer their volunteers educational and enrichment opportunities, in addition to the benefits of being in the company of like-minded individuals who love growing greener cities.

Some communities encourage people to nurture plants in nearby tree boxes or parking strips (also known as the road verge or hellstrip). These areas are often neglected and in need of some attention. Since the soils there are often compacted and poor in nutrients, select tough plants such as yucca, iris, or daylilies that can withstand these conditions and the full sun.

If you are lucky enough to have a green space, but are pushing up against the boundaries and want to add more plantings, look at what is surrounding you. One way to expand is to test spilling out onto the sidewalk. Perhaps place a pot a little over the property line and see how that goes. Be considerate of passersby and tie up anything that will impede foot traffic.

Gardening along back alleys is another option. Approach your neighbors about an alley clean-up and let them know your intentions to beautify the area. Ask them to contribute some plant divisions and to take turns with watering and weeding.

Look for pockets of open ground in your neighborhood that you can adopt as your own. Clear the weeds out, sprinkle some seeds, and give it an occasional watering—this may be all that neglected area needs to thrive.

These little "guerilla gardens" are ephemeral by nature. One day, you may walk by and see your plantings mowed over or suddenly behind a construction fence. That is okay. Such is life. You can always move on and looking for the next pocket garden to maintain.

Color as Accent

It is a shame that so many small-space gardens shy away from color. A garden of all-white flowers is lovely but can also get dull after a while. Mixing in a few hues livens things up and reflects your creativity and personality. If a rainbow of colors is not your thing, think in terms of adding color as an accent.

Perhaps your color accent is seasonal and changing. In spring, cool pastels may reign, but in summer hot tropical colors may dominate. Many gardeners switch out their bulb plantings each year to try out a new palette. For example, bright red and yellow tulips one year and pinks and purples the next.

A signature accent color is pleasing for small-space gardens, where many competing elements can be distracting. Once you decide on that signature color, layer in a couple complementary hues to balance it out. Knowing your signature palette can help you when shopping for plants and furnishings,

but you don't need to limit yourself so strictly. A few spots of contrasting colors can bring a feeling of energy and realness to a garden space. You also don't want to be too "matchy-matchy" or forced.

Neutral colors in the garden include gray, silver, white, black, and all shades from tan to brown. These will be your background and supporting players. Green can act as both a neutral background and be a signature color depending on its hue.

Note that colors can be dark or bright in tone as well. Darker colors can make a small space feel larger as well as more calming and serene. Brighter tones advance toward the viewer and are more stimulating and engaging. Your personal taste and garden theme or style will lead you to one side of the spectrum or the other.

Color can be introduced through your plant foliage and blooms, but also from your hardscape and accessories. Pillows and pots can be color-coordinated as well as outdoor rugs, light fixtures, and bird baths.

Apply your signature accent color to door and window trim or a garden gate. Paint your accent color on a trellis or fence. Splash it on an accent wall. Finally, feel free to play. Paint is relatively cheap and easy to switch if you get bored with the look.

Defensive Tactics for Urban Gardeners

There are many benefits and joys around small-space and urban gardening. However, the reality is that there are some unique challenges to this kind of gardening as well. Most urban gardeners at one time or another encounter theft or destruction. This can be heart-breaking—after all, you have worked hard to create a little oasis in the city, and it can feel so unfair to have that work damaged or stolen.

Urban gardeners should protect themselves as best they can to minimize this and know also that *you are not alone*. When someone steps on your flowers or steals a juicy, ripe tomato, we feel your pain!

A first line of defense is literally a fence. If local rules allow it, install a wall between your garden and passersby so they are not tempted to reach in and help themselves to your blooms and produce. If permanent structures are not allowed, you can construct temporary barriers out of tall containers, several trellises, or freestanding fence panels.

Prickly or thorny plants can also be used as an outer layer for your garden borders to keep people from cutting through and damaging other more delicate plants.

One technique used successfully by urban food growers is to plant the less tempting vegetables to the outside and the more prized ones towards the interior, where they can be hidden by foliage and other plants. In general, large fruiting plants like eggplants, melons, and squash are stolen more than foliage plants like chard, kale, and onions. Mixing edibles into your ornamental flower beds and containers is another good way to disguise them.

Another technique is to grow varieties that are smaller or less recognizable as being "ripe" to others. These include mini peppers and green tomatoes. You can also plant food crops that are exotic or less known in your region. Pick produce as soon as possible so it doesn't look like you do not care or that it is going to waste.

Enlist your neighbors to be your eyes and ears and install a small security camera, if necessary. It is also nice to allow part of your garden to be a "free" area, grown for sharing. For example, you can spread the word to a few households on your block that you have extra fresh herbs should anyone need them.

Finally, try placing a few carefully worded (and waterproof) signs around your garden. Telling your neighbors that the tall blooms along the sidewalk are there for supporting pollinators, may help them understand your choices better and decrease the number of flowers that are stolen. Signs can also help educate and explain individual plants that people might be curious about.

Pet-Friendly Urban Yards

For many people, pets are a part of our families. The need for them to gather with us as we enjoy our landscapes is important. A landscape that is safe and inviting for our four-legged friends requires us to consider the layout a bit differently.

Minimizing turf is simply a great idea. Pet urine can make a lawn unsightly. Unsightly yellow spots can be flushed out with water to dilute the acidity. Using pulverized lime will often help neutralize these spots. Reseeding and repatching at the appropriate time of year for your hardiness zone is also a terrific way to keep the lawn green. When this is not possible, consider installing hardscaping which also provides your pet with alternatives to freely navigating the space.

Pathways should help your pet maneuver throughout the garden. Most pets create a well-traveled path which can often lead to them trampling planted areas. This can make planting a challenge. Learn how to work with your pet to make the space enjoyable for all. Use gravel or stone dust to create easy care pathways for your pet to enjoy. Stone dust has been known to reduce pet odors in the garden which is an added benefit. Replenishing these pathways from time to time is more cost effective than replacing plants repeatedly.

Consider creating a space specifically used by pets to relieve themselves. Use materials that are easy to clean in these areas. Sand can be used for cats. You can train cats to go only where the sand box or designated area is. If you have a dog that loves to dig, create a sand pit that is in an out-of-the-way area where your pet can happily dig away without doing any damage. Hiding treats or bones in the sand area will appease your dog's desire to dig.

Make certain there are areas where your pet has readily available access to water. Leave bowls of water discretely in areas near shade. This will help the water stay cool and encourage the dog to seek shelter from the hot sun, in addition to making time for a drink. A kiddie pool is also a great idea. Your dog will love the opportunity to play in the water on really hot days. Make sure the water is regularly emptied and refreshed to maintain a healthy environment for your pet.

Of course, creating a dog run that is discretely placed in the garden is also a terrific idea. Traditionally, dog runs are known to be ugly chain-link fenced areas. Creatively complement your garden by using materials that help conceal these dog run areas. It is easy to use plant material to hide fencing or to conceal a mulched area that will not be seen. Consider using large, paneled cattle fencing and coordinate this with other existing hardscaped areas. Showing a dog that this is the area for them can make all the difference in how they respect the garden.

Also, if our four-legged friends, such as cats, cannot find a comfortable spot to squat, they will move on to another area. So, insert sturdy twigs in spaces where they are known to repeatedly use. This will discretely encourage them to go elsewhere. The twigs will go unnoticed to the human eye if plant material grows over, as well as around them.

Concealing Unkempt Areas

Unkept areas are commonplace in the urban garden. Finding room to store everything away is sometimes hard. There are a few ways to conceal areas that might otherwise be considered a visual distraction. Whether in a side yard, or at the rear of the garden, release your creativity and find ways to conceal these behind-the-scenes areas.

Our natural inclination is to fence the area in. Fencing is usually the first thing that comes to mind. A short fence seems to disappear into the landscape. Depending on what is being concealed, this is the practical solution. A natural wood fence will weather over time and eventually will need to be replaced. Sometimes the weathering of the wood can be a distraction, however painting it can offer the effect of a colorful screen. Using a vine is sometimes all that is needed to liven up a barren fence.

Planting evergreen shrubs can create a living border that can block out the unkempt area. Depending on the shrub, maintenance is important. Evergreens can sometimes become too large and encroach upon the rest of the garden. Investigate all the options to find the correct cultivar of evergreen shrub to fit your garden. Many new cultivars of evergreen shrubs, as well as trees, have been developed for use in smaller spaces.

Perennial and annual plantings should also be considered. These planted areas add an artistic flair and are great at covering up unsightly areas in the yard. A seasonal perennial planting of various heights, textures, and colors always livens up a yard. When considering perennial plantings, remember that at some point they will need to be divided and transplanted. Choosing well-behaved plant material is always a wise decision. It is important to know what the initial reason is for including a plant as a barrier or a screen. Determining if it should be included in the garden to provide a colorful distraction to hide an unkempt area can be the deciding factor.

When gaps are left in the garden for the year after year planting of annuals, the combinations are endless. Using annuals sometimes also brings the possibilities of having self-seeding plants. These plants can fill a garden throughout the season without having to do any replanting. This will also provide a naturalistic effect which is quite effective for hiding unkempt spaces without being too obvious. Using annuals also presents the opportunity for saving some seed for future use. Redistributing annuals where you want them creates an evolving color and structural visual experience.

Grasses with seasonal interest should also be considered. Depending on the cultivars selected, ornamental grasses offer seasonal interest which can help conceal problematic areas. When the grasses die back, the foliage becomes a point of interest—even in the winter, if left standing. Variegated foliage is often used to add interest and can be effective in drawing the eye away from the unkempt area. Ornamental grasses are an effective, low-cost way to camouflage less-than-perfect areas. As the foliage grows throughout the season and seed heads appear, scruffy areas become less noticeable. Consider using diverse plant material or even hardscaping to provide many different options to conceal those untidy areas.

Creating Vignettes and Focal Points

Small gardens should be treated similarly to inside spaces. These garden rooms need to be created with the same principles as are used in interior design. The key rule of interior design is to create a main focal point that the space centers (and flows) around, then the rest of the room can be decorated with additional distinct vignettes or visual snapshots to create pleasing moments of rest for the eye.

In a formal garden, the layout would be on an axis and the main focal point will be in the dead center. For instance, picture a courtyard with two main paths in an X-pattern or a plus sign (+) pattern with a water fountain at the very center. Side paths could radiate off that center point. On the side paths, there may be large urn-shaped containers sitting on a pedestal at each corner or where one path meets another.

In a less formal garden, the main focal point can be placed off to one side. The paths may be winding or circular. In this style, the vignettes can happen at uneven intervals throughout the garden.

There are many choices for a garden room focal point that include large containers, water features, an ornamental or flowering tree, a seating area, or a piece of garden art. (See Art in the Garden on page 146 and Water Features to Disguise Sound Pollution on page 130.)

Once you choose your garden room's focal point and style (informal or formal), you can start adding in your vignettes. These vignettes are like a still life painting produced in three dimensions. They should be smaller and of less visual importance than your main focal point but can still be captivating and beautiful on their own.

Vignettes can be groupings of planters of varying heights and of complimentary colors. (See Coordinating a Pot Palette on page 176.) A grouping can also be made of non-plant materials such as a tray artfully arranged with several seashells or interesting rocks.

A single, striking container placed into a planting bed can be a lovely vignette and also solve the problem of having a blank space where a planting has yet to fill in.

Charming vignettes can be created by imitating a point in time. For instance, a vignette may be a table set up with a tea service or a potting bench set up with all the planting materials ready to go including a pair of gloves and trowel placed just so—as if the gardener had just stepped away for a moment.

Draw visitors into the garden by creating a comfortable nook with seating in it. Include a few throw pillows and set out a table with glasses and a pitcher of water.

A main focal point makes a small garden feel intentional, and adding vignette moments to it allows the gardener to create a welcoming landscape.

Water Storage Tricks

Access to water is not always available in small-space gardens. If you have a nearby spigot or hose, count yourself as fortunate. For many gardeners, all water used in the garden must be hand-carried in or collected on-site.

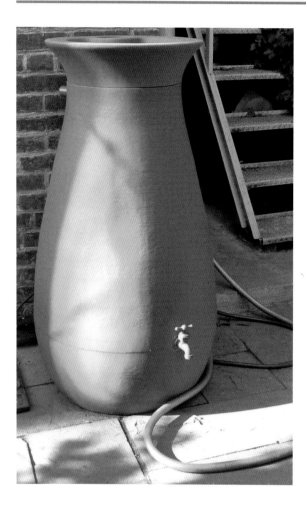

You can temporarily store water in clean milk or juice jugs with lids. Another handy method for those in apartments is to have a small hose that attaches to an indoor sink that you can thread through an open window and then run it out to your balcony or patio when you need to water plants.

A rain barrel is the best choice to collect and store water for your garden. It can be freestanding but is even better if you can place it at the bottom of a downspout. You will want to fit it with a screen across the top. This prevents leaves and other detritus from getting inside. It also acts as a safeguard against small children, pets, or wildlife getting trapped inside.

The barrel should be made from food-grade materials. Although you are not going to drink from it directly, your plants are and some of these you may end up eating yourself.

Barrels come in various sizes and shapes. Some are able to be stacked or linked together for extra or overflow storage.

To use the water in the barrel, you may need to install a spigot and raise the barrel up on blocks so that gravity assists in draining the water out. Otherwise, you can open the top and dip in a watering can.

To prevent mosquitoes from breeding in your stored water, you can use it up the next day or drain the water every few days. You can also sprinkle pellets or put dunks into the water that contain Bti, a bacterium toxic only to mosquito larvae.

You will need to drain and store the barrel upside down in the winter if you live in a cold climate. This is true for anything that holds water that is subject to freezing—including your watering cans and any containers not holding plants during the cold months.

A cistern is a great choice if you can bury it before you create your landscape or you have additional space available, such as under a deck. This works similarly to a rain barrel, but you will need to also install a pump to extract the water to use it.

Tool Storage Tips

Small gardens often suffer from a lack of storage space. You may find your garden tools, gloves, and soil bags piling up in various spots where you last used them, or worse, sitting inside your home. "A place for everything and everything in its place" has no truer meaning than in a tiny garden.

The key to good storage is finding a space that is out of view, but still easily accessible. You won't use it if it's hard to get to. In addition, storing things out in the open can be hard on your tools and other gardening supplies. Metal tools in particular can rust and wood handles will decay more quickly when exposed to the elements.

One clever storage option is a garden bench that can serve dual purposes as seating and storing items inside. These can be purchased or made by you. An old bench can also be adapted and used as a bit of shelter for a drawer or trunk on wheels that can slide underneath it.

If you have the space for a narrow potting bench or shed, these can be maximized by adding extra shelves and hooks. A square metal grid or pegboard tacked above an old side table can serve as an impromptu potting area. You can hang s-hooks from the grid to hold small tools, and buckets placed under the table can hold soils, fertilizers, etc.

An old baker's rack is a terrific solution. It has plenty of flat surfaces and hanging areas already built into its design. These are often available for a nominal price at secondhand stores.

When you are storing things in a small garden, neatness counts. Look for ways to neatly stack like items together. When a large container is not in use, it can double as storage space for smaller items like plant labels, twine, and stakes.

If you are fortunate enough to have a garage or other outbuilding to use, you can install a hanging rack and create a storage wall for large hand tools like rakes and hoes. Getting tools up and off the ground helps to prevents accidents.

Another trick is to create a low wall around your storage area. This can be created by planting some medium to tall shrubs to disguise it. Or you can install a section of permanent fencing that blocks the area from outside view.

A large basket or tote by your entrance can store your most used gardening items such as pruners, a trowel, and gloves. If you find yourself constantly going back and forth to retrieve tools to use, think about installing a mailbox or other enclosed bin in a few separate spots and storing duplicate tools in them to save you the extra steps and time searching for what you need to get the job done.

Bonus tip: If you are forever losing your tools in the garden. Paint the handles a bright color that will show up when they are left among your plants.

Joy in Repetition

Small-space gardens are like little jewel boxes or treasure chests. In these contained areas, you can discover endless treasures and delights. Because your focus is limited to one spot, you can experience things in detail and in-depth.

One principle to maximize a small-space garden is to repeat of certain design elements. Patterns and repetition in a small garden can be used to great effect to please the eye and soul. Our human brains crave the sensation of making sets and matches—putting puzzles together and matching like-with-like.

To take advantage of this in a small space, you can start by coordinating your containers. (See Coordinating a Pot Palette on page 176.) Next, look at the hardscape elements in your surroundings. In a typical unplanned space, you might have a brick wall, a stone path, a concrete patio, and a wooden fence, but consider the impact if you were to change one or more of these materials to match each other. To do that you can replace the path with brick or add a stone surface to the patio. The least expensive option would be to paint the fence and patio or wall in the same tones. Give it some thought and maybe create a multi-year plan to upgrade and coordinate your hardscapes as you are able.

Next, evaluate your furnishings. Perhaps you have a wooden table and a mix of metal and plastic chairs. Decide what material you prefer in the long run and then swap out the furnishings as your budget allows.

The smaller decorative pieces are your next area of focus and not only are they the easiest to switch out, but they can have the biggest immediate impact. These can range from outdoor throw pillows to rugs to watering cans and tools.

A can of spray paint can go a long way in touching up various worn-out finishes and sprucing things up. You can pick one color to be your signature color and use it everywhere or you can pick two or three colors to contrast and highlight different ornamental items with them. One easy project is painting several small birdhouses in the same color (or repeating two or three colors) and then hanging them in a row along a wall or fence line.

The final elements that can be repeated to pleasing effect are your plantings. You can have a signature plant that you use in several different spots in the planting beds and in containers. This is a lovely way to lead visitors' eyes around your garden in a guided way. You can also repeat certain combinations and patterns in your plantings that will create an "ah-ha" moment of recognition in the mind of the garden observer.

A garden with repeated design elements is one that engages the visitor as well. It subliminally says to them that care and planning were put into the space and this promotes a warm and welcoming atmosphere.

Paths and Walkways

In a tightly spaced garden, leaving ample space for walkways can seem like a low priority use of valuable gardening real estate. A common mistake made by beginning gardeners is to make the paths as narrow as possible between their garden beds. You will thank yourself in future years if you install more generous pathways right from the start so you won't have to go back and rip out your established beds and redo them.

Wide paths will allow you to use a wheelbarrow to add soil amendments to the beds. They also will accommodate garden visitors with a variety of mobility levels from toddlers to seniors. Wider walks are better for viewing your garden, taking in all the plantings and seeing the overall design.

When situating a walkway, stay at least 2 to 3 feet (60 to 100 cm) away from nearby trees so their root systems don't push up through the path. Also look at how the water drains during a rainstorm. You can use the pathway to help with that drainage by having it angle in one direction. You want to avoid water pooling on your paths.

Paths and walkways can be simple strips of turfgrass that are the width of a mower. These are popular in temperate climates. If your pathways are planted with turf or other types of walkable groundcovers, you will want to edge them to create a defining break between the paths and planting beds to make the latter easier to weed. (See Bed Edging Options on page 148.)

Pavers with grass or other plants placed among them are another great option. Pavers interplanted with low-growing herbs can be quite lovely and you have the bonus effect of having a scent released as you travel the path. (See Groundcovers as Lawn Alternatives on page 86.)

You can place slate pieces or stepping stones on the ground, trace them with a trowel, and then dig out their silhouette. Finally, replace the stone or slate back in the depression. These will be slightly raised above the soil surface to start with, but after several years you will find they are level with the surrounding ground and maybe even sink lower. At that point, you might dig them out and backfill in the depression to raise them again.

Some people like the pleasing crunch of walking on the surface of a gravel, pebble, or crushed shell pathway. This type of path is fairly easy to install, but requires future maintenance as weeds love to take advantage of this open area because it offers full sun and great drainage.

An elegant brick or stone pathway is a little more work, though worth it for creating a smooth and even walking surface. For this you will need bricks, a border, sand, and a base material. Dig out the area, fill it with the base material, grade it, tamp it down, add a sand layer, and then tamp it again. Next, set the bricks along the edge and then fill in the interior pattern. Finally, fill the gap between the bricks with sand or stone dust.

Whatever surface material you choose, mapping out and including garden paths and walkways can elevate your small garden into a well-planned and ordered space.

Creating a Borrowed View

A borrowed view can make even the smallest garden become much more interesting. The average urban garden is usually small to medium in size and so using a borrowed view can give the feeling of being in a larger garden. Creating a landscape that has an interesting view can easily be accomplished. Using the proper plants, you can start by creating an enticing invitation to enter the garden. Once there, plants can lead the eye to an expanded view. The view is not just what is visible right in front of you, but also includes what is beyond, or sometimes what is even out of sight.

By creating vertical focal points, the garden now has immediate interest enticing visitors to look upward. If the site is semi-shady and protected, consider a medium-height understory tree. Interesting branching or a diverse leaf structure offer a reason to look up into, and sometimes through, the canopy.

Consider choosing a columnar or narrow evergreen for a sunny site. These shrubs or small trees require minimal maintenance and will reward you by being a garden focal point year-round. Perhaps a four-season tree that is hardy for your gardening zone should be considered. Consider selecting one that will provide colorful new growth in the spring, followed by brilliant blooms in the summer, attractive fall foliage, and distinctive bark in the winter. On some trees, the blooms are sometimes followed by seed pods that hang on the branches like ornaments—which are decorative and also feed the winter birds. Placement of these trees so they draw the eye outward is important so visitors take notice of the broader landscape view.

For trees that also have peeling bark or strikingly colorful foliage, they are very useful to attract attention during the winter months. These trees often become more beautiful over time. Creatively pruning the branches can help draw the eye to a specific area of the garden as well. Often these trees cast interesting shadows on the ground as well, drawing the eye downward to perhaps discover a path beckoning onward. Turning a bend to look around a well-placed tree can often lead to a very different view.

Keeping the size of trees and shrubs in proportion with the home is critical. In a smaller yard, consider planting a small tree or tall shrub that averages about 5 to 7 feet (1.5 to 2 m) tall. This size, up to a maximum of about 10 feet (3 m) is a good palatable size for ease of maintenance as well as providing a balanced canopy that is not too wide. Deciding on the focal point is merely the beginning of a memorable view. The underplanting below draws the eye downward and beyond, offering attractive vignettes to redirect the eye.

Consider including spots of green (with a twist) to the garden. This pop of green can add an accent right where you need a bit of pizzaz. Textural and even monotone green foliage does have added value throughout the garden. Variegated or brilliantly colored foliage is a great way to draw the eye to different parts of the garden. Adding ornamental grasses at the edge of a landscape (and even dotted within) offers movement and encourages visitors to look beyond what is right at their feet. Adding a few of these elements will often make a small space look bigger.

Look beyond the obvious and imagine yourself entering a different garden within your existing garden. By doing this you can achieve an interesting view from multiple angles. As the season evolves, stellar plant material, whether annual or perennial and even shrubs and trees, can lead the eyes to quite the interesting, borrowed view.

Guide Visitors by Framing the View

The views into a small garden space can be framed—literally and figuratively—to lead visitors to the areas that you want them to see and to distract them from less-attractive spots.

Perhaps, you have a jumble of power lines in back of your garden or a messy back-alley area where the trash bins are stored. These can be screened in various ways. (See Structures for Screening on page 122.) Still, these are not the first spots you want friends and family to notice when they drop by for a visit.

By guiding views through the use of framing, you set up powerful sightlines that lead your visitors to your garden's highlights. Your garden should have several spots where the eye can rest and take in a planned scene. (See Creating Vignettes and Focal Points on page 165.)

Framing can be as simple as a freestanding archway. Vines can be planted at the base and guided up and over each side of the arch. Or the arch can be left free of greenery—especially if it is an attractive shape or color.

A frame can be two trellises or other tall structures located on each side of a path that stand as sentinels to guide the way. These two sentinels might also be two large, tall planters or two small trees—anything that creates the look and feel of two guards standing watch at an entranceway.

You can literally place a large window or door in a garden to create a framed view. Windows can be hung or placed in a freestanding holder. The door will need bracing, staking, or some kind of support system to keep it upright.

Frames can be made by training plants into an archway shape or planting a dense layer or hedge with an opening pruned into it that spotlights the garden's main focal point or a specific vignette.

Garden gates are a terrific way to frame a view. Whether left open all the time or closed to create a sense of mystery, the gate offers a framed view that should be planned to unfold for the visitor, even before they step through it.

Asian-style gardens incorporate framed views as an essential part of their designs. (See Asian-Themed Garden on page 99.) The classic moon gate is a popular feature in many of them. They also use framed views that are incorporated through garden outbuildings such as a tea house or shed.

Don't forget to also frame the views of the garden that you see looking out into it from inside your home. Sit at each garden-facing window and sketch out the plantings that you currently see and then plan for how you might enhance these vistas. Think about how they might change over the seasons as well.

Finally, evaluate the entryways into your home. A well-curated porch or front door planting is an essential way to "frame the view" for visitors to your garden. (See Inviting Doorways and Entryways on page 76.)

Coordinating a Pot Palette

Have you ever entered a garden or room and been unsettled by the jumble of different materials and colors being used? Coordinating your collection of planters, pots, and containers can give your small-space garden a cohesive feel. (See Joy in Repetition on page 169.)

Coordinating your containers can start by matching the materials they are created from. You can choose from plastic, terra cotta, wood, metal, ceramic, stone, concrete, or glass—but not all of them.

Don't dismiss plastic out-of-hand as "looking cheap." Many of today's plastic planters are very high-quality containers. They can look sleek and modern or be shaped and textured to imitate other natural materials. You may find yourself at the garden center knocking on the side of a pot to detect if it is actually made of stone or terra cotta—only to realize that it is made of high-quality plastic.

Plastic has the benefit of being lightweight and typically is less expensive than other container materials. It is also a good material for holding in moisture and insulating plant roots. If you live in an area with harsh winters, you may want to use

more durable plastic pots that have a double-wall construction. This provides an insulating layer of air between the outer edge and the soil inside to protect overwintering plants.

Other container materials have their pros and cons. Terra cotta is good for growing plants that like excellent drainage like herbs and succulents. Wood is inexpensive, but not long-lasting. Metal is distinctive but can heat up in the summer sun. Stone is beautiful, but very heavy. Ceramic is attractive but can crack and break in cold climates.

Once you choose your preferred material, then choose your color palette. Some gardeners prefer all neutrals or earth tones so the containers visually disappear and the plants are the featured element. Others may prefer a modern or traditional pot palette of white, black, and/or gray containers that lend an elegant effect.

And then there are those gardeners that love to work with color. Here you can be more playful and creative. You can collect containers in primary or pastel tones. You can also have a tight color theme or go crazy and have many shades of one hue. This is about personal expression and what pleases your eye.

One popular choice for colorful containers are the deep-blue ceramic ones—related to these are the light green, aqua, or cerulean planters. These tones of blues and greens are lovely paired with all kinds of plant foliage combinations. They can be used to accentuate the yellow-veining pattern in a leaf or the gray-green color of succulent stems.

Your planters are an investment and good ones can be expensive. Gardeners often gift themselves with a new, choice planter each year at the start of the season or on their birthday to slowly build up their collection. Take care of them and they will reward you with years of enjoyment in your garden.

Mirrors to Give Depth and Increase Light

Let's reflect on all the great things there are about small-space gardens. First, the limited space teaches you to edit and be more selective in your plant and design choices. You can narrow things down to your favorites and those items of the best quality. Next, small spaces allow you to focus on a specific aspect of your surroundings and enjoy all parts of it. Finally, a garden space with restricted boundaries frees you to explore other avenues of gardening rather than just having time to do the constant maintenance and upkeep of a larger space.

Given all these small-space benefits, one aspect that you might long to improve upon is enhancing the sense of depth for your space. A tight area can lead to feeling closed-in or claustrophobic. To alleviate that, try the careful placement of mirrors.

In addition to adding depth, mirrors can bounce light back into a space. Use them to reflect the sun, and any artificial light sources, back into the garden to brighten up a dark corner. Be careful, of course, that a mirror's concentrated reflected light is not so strong or at such an angle as to burn your plants or furnishings (especially if it is a concave mirror). Test different placements out before you hang or mount the mirror.

Mirrors can come in various forms and shapes. It could be a vintage framed piece or a mirrored drinks tray. You can create a mirror by purchasing reflective glass, cutting it to size, adding a frame, and putting a hanger or handles on it. You can also breathe new life into an old mirror by resilvering it yourself or having a professional do it for you.

Because the mirror will be exposed to the outdoor elements, using one that is old or has a worn finish with some scratches or imperfections on it is just fine. You might give it a good cleaning to freshen it up periodically, but the aging process can be part of its attraction in a wabi-sabi kind of way.

A larger mirror placed at the end of a pathway is an old trick used to make the space feel larger. Plant vines around it to cover the edges and the illusion will fool even you after a few years of plant growth takes place.

A quick and easy way to add mirrored surfaces into your garden beds is with a reflective gazing ball. These can be placed on the ground or set on a pedestal. They can also be hung from nearby tree limbs. These shiny glass balls were originally used to ward off evil spirits and bring good luck. Today, gazing balls are a decorative element to reflect back the beauty of the garden to appreciative eyes gazing upon them.

Composting in a Metal Garbage Can

Not everyone has space for a compost pile or a place to store the resulting composted materials. Some local ordinances also may prohibit open composting from happening for fear of attracting pests. Luckily, creating compost in a metal garbage can is easy to do on a patio, balcony, or back alley.

Select a metal trash can with a tight-fitting lid. A bungee cord and/or weight on the top can be used for added protection against clever vermin. Simply drill holes about 6 to 12 inches (15 to 30 cm) apart all around the trash can on the sides, bottom, and lid.

Place the can on a surface that is stable and also will allow for good drainage. If possible, put a few bricks underneath to permit air circulation under the can as well.

Chop up food scraps and plant material to the smallest possible size to speed up the composting process inside the can. A handful of nitrogen-rich fertilizer or compost activator can be added as well to give the process a boost.

Mix in both "green" and "brown" materials so the pile does not get too wet or too dry. Green materials include produce past its prime, weeds, and grass clippings. Brown materials include woody stems of plants, leaves, and shredded paper.

The key to creating good compost is mixing in oxygen and water. Turn the composting materials inside the can every day or so by laying the can on its side and rolling it a few times. The more you mix the materials, the faster the decay and break down will happen. If the mix is too dry, add some water as needed.

Do not compost weeds with mature seeds on them. Your small compost system cannot heat up enough to kill the seeds and you don't want to inadvertently add them back into your garden. Be careful also about adding in diseased plant material as that can spread the problem back into your garden as well.

The volume of the composting materials will shrink over several weeks. If you add more materials to it, the compost will take longer to finish. For this reason, some home composters have several cans going at various stages to speed up the process.

CHAPTER 10

Supporting Urban Wildlife

GARDENING HAS INCREASED our interest in making sure we help our local wildlife to thrive. Each year an increasing amount of land is used for building homes and commercial buildings. This disrupts the habitats of our urban wildlife—the natural world that helps keep our ecosystem in balance.

There are ways to ensure that wildlife can survive. We can do this by creating habitats that provide housing, food, and shelter that fit right into our urban garden landscapes. Planting more native species will offer food, as well as materials for wildlife housing. Creating protective spaces where wildlife can overwinter safely is important as well. Including elements in the garden which support urban wildlife, while maintaining an aesthetically pleasing landscape, is easier than you think.

Providing Nectar, Fruits & Seeds for Wildlife

Providing plant material to sustain wildlife in the urban garden is easier than you think. Butterflies, birds, and even bumblebees need to have a reliable source of nutrition to survive. There are many plants that can aid in attracting them and also provide nutrition for them, as well as add beauty to the urban garden.

One beautiful benefit of an urban landscape is the ability to notice nature up close. Watching wildlife eat in your garden is a very rewarding experience. First, make certain that you provide water. Water is one of the easiest items to include in the urban garden. A simple, shallow dish slightly tilted with a few rocks or a mound of sand in it provides a place for wildlife to pause and drink. When placed out of harm's way, the dish will allow birds and butterflies to take advantage of a place to drink as they pass through the garden.

Consider using plants that provide nectar to attract birds and butterflies. There are many trees, shrubs, perennials, and even annuals from which to choose. There are plants with nectar-filled blooms for any size of the space. Adding them will attract most nectar-seeking wildlife. Hummingbirds are known to prefer bright, tubular blooms. If you are limited on space, try using a pot or planter with annuals that will soon be the site for a bit of wildlife theater. Watching the birds as well as the butterflies will provide countless hours of entertainment. A few plants that have nectar-filled blooms to consider are:

- Wild bergamot or bee balm *(Monarda fistulosa)*
- Summersweet *(Clethra alnifolia)*
- Purple coneflower *(Echinacea purpurea)*
- Elderberry *(Sambucus* sp.)

Fruiting plants will also bring in birds, in addition to other forms of wildlife such as squirrels, foxes, and even racoons. There are many native trees like the oaks *(Quercus* sp.) that will provide beauty as well as be a host for beneficial insects. Other trees, in all sizes, that provide fruit for wildlife include:

- Cherry, peach, almond, or plum *(Prunus* sp.)
- Shadbush or serviceberry *(Amelanchier* sp.)
- Red mulberry *(Morus rubra)*
- Maples *(Acer* sp.)

Seeds of all sizes can provide nutritious food for wildlife in the urban garden. Watching birds visit a window birdfeeder that is filled with seed from sunflowers and other plants can be rewarding. During the warmer months, certain plants might attract bees and butterflies. When autumn arrives, consider leaving the garden slightly unkempt. Allowing seed heads to remain in place at the end of the season can provide wildlife with the necessary nutritious treats they need to survive the winter. There are even birds that will stay in the garden and need this food to survive the winter. A few plants that provide seeds that are eaten by the birds are:

- Dill *(Anethum graveolens)*
- Fennel *(Foeniculum vulgare)*
- Milkweed *(Asclepias* sp.)
- Violets *(Viola* sp.)
- Goldenrod *(Solidago* sp.)
- Coneflower or black-eyed Susans *(Rudbeckia* sp.)

Providing stems, seed heads, and berries for wildlife at the end of the season will also provide protection during the colder months. When we provide the proper necessities for a safe haven, we are protecting our wildlife. In the urban garden, watching nature thrive is a wonderful return on any plant investment.

Hotels and Habitats

Creating habitats and nesting areas for beneficial insects and amphibians can become quite the adventure. One easy way to create a habitat is by allowing plant debris to remain in the garden during the winter months. Some beneficial insects love burrowing underground. So consider leaving at least half of the prior seasons' plant debris standing in the garden to provide an extra layer of protection for the overwintering insects. This will provide the perfect setting to entice beneficial insects to move in.

Purchasing an insect hotel is another way to add a nesting or hibernating site. Usually, these beneficial insect habitats are colorful, offer many nooks, and can be mounted anywhere in the garden. Make certain that you can clean the inside of the hotel so you protect the inhabitants from disease and intruders like parasitic wasps. A thorough cleaning should become common practice at least once a year.

The fun part of attracting beneficial insects and amphibians is creating your own unique habitat from scratch. You can create a habitat by using leftover wood, pallets, cinder (cement) blocks, and bricks. Most of these items can be readily found nearby or are quite affordable to purchase. Also, consider collecting straw, pinecones, ornamental grass debris, sticks, cardboard, and even clay chimney liners for your insect habitat area. Be creative when collecting debris for the habitats. You do not have to go far to find things like leftover tree limbs that can be cut to fit. The older tree limbs are a perfect spot to drill holes for insect nesting sites.

Siting the habitat is also important. A sunny spot that will warm up on cold winter days naturally will be appreciated by many beneficial insects. Make certain the structure has a roof to provide protection from strong winds and rain. Some habitat structures can be anchored to an existing wall and created with legs so they are freestanding. They can even be situated on a raised area in the rear or side in the garden.

Proportional sizing is important to consider so the habitat will not overwhelm the garden space. First create a frame for your habitat. A freestanding frame should minimally be 6 to 8 inches (15 to 20 cm) deep. Create sections or nooks in a manner that is pleasing to the eye. If a freestanding habitat is chosen, make certain the rear is closed to keep the ingredients securely in place. Fill each nook with collected items (listed above) that will offer a diverse range of nesting possibilities.

When creating a habitat for beneficial insects and amphibians such as toads and frogs, using pallets or found wood is a great foundation or starting point. Creating levels on the foundation with various materials will attract a multitude of guests. Perhaps add old unused clay pots filled with small pinecones, acorn tops, or even magnolia cones. Cover the top of the pot with chicken wire or hardware cloth to keep out unwanted guests. Bricks set on their side, holes drilled in old branches, a cluster of various sized pinecones, and even chimney liners filled with hollow straw will provide inviting accommodations for beneficial insects. Nooks of various widths and depths will keep the habitat hotel at full capacity.

Habitat hotels and nesting sites add life to the garden. Attracting beneficial insects and amphibians can ensure our gardens are productive and protected naturally.

Making Wise Native Plant Choices

In recent years, native plant choices have become much easier to find. With a growing awareness to be kinder to the environment, as well the need to provide food sources for the pollinators, using the right native plants is important. Researching native plants and their usefulness in the landscape has increased awareness about incorporating them into our urban gardens. There are a few things to consider when selecting native plants.

A native plant is usually a plant that has thrived in a specific area naturally for over thousands of years. Plants that are bred (cultivars) from these hardy specimens are called nativars. Nativars generally have the hardiness of a native plant, with a genetic difference. Between the native parents and the nativar offspring, there might be increased disease resistance, new colors, differences in height variances, and more.

Another grouping of plants to recognize are the naturalized plants. An example of a naturalized plant is the orange daylily (*Hemerocallis fulva*). This plant, originally from China, has naturalized throughout much of the United States and parts of Canada. It is frequently seen along roadsides, fields, and more. This plant is beautiful, multiplies quickly, but has been known to overtake native vegetation. Knowing which native, nativar, or naturalized plant to choose is very important.

What is your planting zone? This is an important factor in plant selection. Tolerance of temperature highs and lows can vary from plant to plant. Some plants may be native to a warmer or cooler climate than your garden. These natives might not fare well in your hardiness zone conditions.

Site selection is the next important factor when choosing a native plant. Are you seeking to include native plants into the existing landscape that already has non-natives in it or create a bed specifically for native plants? Adding natives into the existing landscape requires research. Some plants are capable of adapting into conditions that are not fully compatible with their original growing climate. Although they will often grow under a new set of environmental conditions, these conditions might inhibit the plant's spread or allow them to grow well beyond its boundaries.

The native perennial, Joe-Pye weed (*Eutrochium fistulosum*) is quite beautiful. In its natural habitat, it grows along roadsides in North America. In this native setting, it can lean on neighboring grasses as well as provide food and cover for wildlife. Its boundaries can be limitless in a moist, rich natural setting. This native plant can be quite tall and aggressive in some regions and might not be suitable for incorporating into an existing garden. In the urban garden, perhaps its shorter nativar cousin, *Eutrochium dubium* 'Baby Joe', might be better used as a substitute.

Know which plant you are thinking to incorporating into your garden. If it is a nativar, find out if it will perform as well as the native plant. Some nativars will not provide what the pollinators need. Make certain that your plant choice is a beneficial resource for the pollinators, as well as native to your region.

Consider consulting local resources to find out more about your native plants. A reputable local nursery will know what plants thrive in the region where you live. Also, reach out to local native plant societies for regional information. A diverse landscape that incorporates native plants and non-native plants is a wise way to garden.

Nesting Sites and Water

Even the smallest gardens can support local wildlife. When a green space is in close proximity to lots of humans and nearby busy roads, it is even more important to give wild creatures little pockets of protective habitats that they can feel safe within.

Our feathered friends are especially appreciative of a private, secluded spot or a nook to raise their young. Birdhouses should be placed far enough up on a wall, fence, or pole to discourage predators from climbing and disturbing them. They should be at least 5 feet (1.5 m) up. However, the birdhouses should not be so high up as to be out of reach. They have to be able to be taken down for cleaning periodically.

Birdhouses should be placed away from the hot afternoon sun. A shady spot behind a large shrub or tree can offer some shelter and the nearby foliage will camouflage the comings and goings of the birds.

Offering nesting material is an additional step you can take to support birds. Nesting materials can include wads of straw, chopped-up and dried grasses, shredded paper, cotton balls, and pine needles. You can stuff these into a small wire cage and hang it out in a sheltered spot for the birds to find.

All wildlife is attracted to fresh, running water. If you can install a recirculating water feature, this will serve both the creatures visiting your garden and as a lovely design element.

If the only water source you can offer is still water, such as in a birdbath, it should be refilled with clean water daily. Daily changes of the water will keep the birdbath clean for the birds and prevent mosquitoes from using it as a breeding ground.

Keep the water shallow as birds do not like to use deep water. When the temperature is so cold that the water might freeze, you can place a solar-powered or battery-operated heater in the water to keep it accessible for use year-round.

Don't be surprised if other creatures aside from the birds use the nesting materials and water sources too. If you are near to a beekeeper with active hives, you may see honey bees lining up on the edge of the birdbath to take a sip as well. Aid them by placing a few rocks and sticks in the water for them to safely land upon.

Butterflies and other beneficial insects also appreciate having a water source. You can create one by partially burying a large, shallow bowl or saucer and then fill it almost to the top with sand or aquarium gravel and a few larger stones for the insects to land on. Finally, slowly pour in water so it is just saturated to the top of the sand or gravel.

CHAPTER 11

Vertical Growing Ideas

URBAN GARDENS ARE usually small to medium sized in stature. This by no means suggests that the actual growing area cannot be maximized well beyond the square footage of the garden. With the right perspective, growing up can add lots of interest at eye level and sometimes even beyond. Utilizing unique structures, arbors, or archways can add a different dimension to any garden space by growing upward.

Supporting structures can be purchased in ready-to-assemble kits. There are also blueprints that are accessible online to create a structure that is uniquely yours. First, there are a few things to consider prior to purchasing or creating a structure to grow plants vertically. How strong will it need to be? Is the structure intended for temporary use or will it become a stationary garden structure? Should it be a statement piece, a form of garden art, or will it become invisible under the climbing plant? Here are a few methods to successfully grow plants vertically in the urban garden.

Ladders and Trellises

Some plants need your help to grow vertically. These are typically vines that would be happy to run all over the ground and take off in all directions without your intervention and training. These rambling plants are happy to scramble wherever you guide them.

A great benefit of growing edible vines on ladders and trellis systems is that it gets the vines off the ground and you are better able to harvest from them. (See Supports and Trellises for Squash and Gourds on page 55.)

Of course, the other main benefit of training vines this way is that it frees up ground space for other plants. A side benefit is that the plants get increased air circulation around them, which can improve the plant's health and cut down on fungal diseases and other issues.

An old wooden ladder is perfect for this purpose—a few broken or missing rungs are just fine. You can always nail in some more rungs if you need them. If the vine you are growing on the ladder has fine tendrils that can't quite grasp around the thick legs and rungs of the ladder, then you can drape a fine mesh netting over it for the plant to cling to.

Other sources for DIY trellises are bamboo poles or long sticks. You can lash three of these at the top to create a stable teepee shape. Be careful if you use any sticks from plants in the willow (*Salix sp.*) family as these can root and regrow easily. This is fine if you want to create a garden shelter, but not so great if they start to grow and shade out the tomatoes that you are training on them!

When using a trellis or support, whether in the ground or in a container, be sure to insert the supports at the same time as you do the initial plantings. If you come back later and stab the supports into the soil where the plants are already growing, you can injure their root system.

Sometimes a vine may need a little coaxing and assistance to find the base of the ladder or trellis and in this case, you can use a bamboo skewer or small stick to start them growing on their way upward.

A strong windstorm can knock over plant supports or even dislodge plants from their support system. If this happens, just gently right everything and put the plants back in place. To prevent the ladder or trellis from tipping over too easily, you can bury the bottom legs or attach ground stakes to them for added stability.

Some climbing or rambling plants do not have tendrils of their own to grasp onto a ladder or trellis. In that case, you need to do the attaching for them. The best materials to do this with are ones that have some give and stretch to them so that they will not rub and injure the vines themselves. You can use strips of old pantyhose or soft plant ties to secure vines or rambling plants to a ladder or trellis.

Rooftop Garden Considerations

With containers, furnishings, and the right plants, you can turn an empty rooftop into a lovely green oasis. There are many benefits to rooftop gardening including access to full sun and 100 percent protection from nibbling deer and rabbits. Before you start lugging pots of soil up to the rooftop though, you will first need to consider several factors.

The first factor to consider is access. If the space is on a commercial building, you will have to contact the building owner and seek permission to build a rooftop garden. You will also want to know who else has access to the space and if it is possible to secure your supplies there. Is there elevator access available or a locked staircase that can be used?

Many rental apartment complexes allow and encourage balcony gardens but may not have thought about sharing the rooftop space. Whether you are a renter or not, good relations with the management is key to maintaining a garden on the rooftop of a building that you do not own. If you are thinking of using the roof on a co-op or condominium association building, you will need to get clearance from the owner's group or board of directors. (While you are at it, why not approach your landlord or owner's group about starting a communal compost pile for the building, holding a balcony garden contest, or allowing a sunny part of the grounds to be converted to community garden plots?)

Once you have permission, your next step will be determining how much weight the roof can handle and whether it is safe to create a garden there. A structural engineer should be able to give you an indication of the rooftop's capability. You want the engineer to factor in not only the weight of the plants, pots, soils, etc., but also of the weight of the water that will be held in those containers, soil, and plant roots. This is a considerable amount and will be a significant factor in the calculations.

Now that you have permission and know you can safely grow up there, your next consideration will be materials—the more lightweight, the better. We recommend using grow bags. These add only a bit of weight and at the end of the growing season can be folded up and easily stored away. (See more about this in chapter 1 on fabric containers and bags.)

To save you from making frequent trips to your indoor faucets with a heavy watering can, you may want to use self-watering containers. (See Self-Watering Containers on page 14.) Other ways to keep your plants hydrated include adding soil moisture gel pellets when you plant them or installing a drip irrigation system strung between your containers connected to a hidden rain barrel.

Next, you will need to account for the additional intense sun, heat, and wind exposure that takes place on rooftops. This may impact your plant selections and placement. For example, plants that are tall and narrow can easily be blown over—even in a light wind. You might place these top-heavy plants against a wall or anchor them to a nearby structure. Another choice would be to weigh down containers with a brick placed in the bottom below the soil level.

Finally, you will want to start small. It's wise to plant just a few pots at a time and then you can add to them as you get comfortable taking on more rooftop garden space. Then, you can consider putting in pavers or tiles, a comfortable seating area, and some other decorative elements. Once you make it your own, that rooftop garden space can provide hours of fun, enjoyment, and relaxation.

Succulents in a Frame

Picture, if you will, a frame filled with different succulent varieties—a play of various colors and textures. This living art can be hung on a wall or fence. It can also be placed on a table surface, or you can create a freestanding frame for it.

Succulents are the perfect choice for vertical growing projects. (You can also try this with Mediterranean herbs or other plants that do well in full sun and like quick-draining soils.)

With this method of vertical growing, you are basically creating a mini-green wall system. You can buy pre-formed wall garden frames and kits or easily create your own. To do so, you will need an old shadow box or frame with some depth to it. (You can also use a shallow box attached to a regular frame.) Next, you will need landscape fabric, hardware cloth, soil, and succulents of your choosing.

Hardware cloth is a sturdy wire mesh with openings of about a centimeter in size. This works better than chicken wire for this project as the openings on chicken wire are generally too large to hold the soil and plants in place.

The soil for this project should be a porous, sandy potting mix designed specifically for cactus and succulents.

You can choose succulents that are winter-hardy in your gardening zone or ones that are annuals and will only last outdoors during the warm months— or a mix of both. If your succulent frame has any non-hardy varieties in it, you will need to replace them each year or you can attempt to overwinter the growing frame indoors.

To construct the project, use a heavy-duty staple gun to attach the hardware cloth inside the frame. Next, cut out some landscape cloth and staple it on the back of the frame—leaving enough space to insert the soil and then finish stapling all around it.

You can now insert your succulents. Strip off their bottom leaves and insert their stems through the hardware cloth and into the soil mix. If they fall out easily, you can use extra wire to hold them in place until they grow their roots and start to grab onto the soil mix.

Water the whole thing and attach a hanger to the back and mount it where you would like it. Depending on your climate and weather, you may need to give the succulents some occasional extra water, but in general they should do fine with what rain they get naturally.

When you start off, you do not need a succulent piece for every opening in the hardware cloth. The fun part of this project is watching how the different succulents grow and fill in the openings around them. Some are faster spreading than others. You may wish to do some editing and moving around as the season progresses.

Espalier for Maximizing Space

Sometimes going "up" is all the choice you have in your small-space garden and other times it is simply a fun technique for maximizing the use of your growing space. Either way, espalier is one method you can use to create more surface area for your plants to expand and use.

Espalier is training a woody plant horizontally against a flat surface such as a wall or fence. This training can be done using a lattice, wire guides, or other support system. In addition to trees and shrubs, this method can also be used to train woody vines.

Training a tree horizontally allows you to have a much wider selection of plant choices available to you. You can play with some varieties that you may not have even considered, because they can grow far too large to be used in a small-space garden. Espalier keeps that growth in check and their size manageable.

Another benefit of espalier is that it gives the plant more reflected warmth from the nearby flat surface. This can be used to a big advantage to grow plants that might be one zone out of your normal hardiness growing range. Examples of plants that are great choices for espalier include pyracantha, magnolia, camellia, and cotoneaster.

Espalier is most often used for training fruit trees against a brick or stone wall. This can increase your productive growing space as well as give the trees some added protection from the elements.

(See Dwarf and Small Fruit Trees on page 59 for more on these type of trees.)

You can purchase plants that are already started on an espalier frame and continue that training, or you can create an espalier system from scratch yourself. To begin, select a woody plant with a central stem or leader and plant it against a wall or fence. Prune back that leader and shoots will emerge from buds along the sides of the main stem. Select the best two shoots and gently attach them to the support wires. Then continue with this pattern until you have the growth you like. To maintain it, simply prune out any growth that is outside of your desired shape.

You can sketch out an espalier pattern on paper for reference or create a grid in advance of training your plant in the pattern you desire. The pattern can be a splayed-open V-shape, crossing Xs, or a series of horizontal Ts. You might even attempt an advanced candelabra shape. There are many patterns to consider. Whichever pattern you choose, this formal training style lets you expand your planting space and practice your pruning creativity.

Planting Pockets on Walls and Fences

Extending the beauty of a garden to the walls and fences can be an exciting challenge. Planting pockets are an easy way to add vertical interest and beauty to a blank area. These pockets can be made of fabric, wood, or plastic. Every year there are more options in size, color, as well as materials that can be used for planting pockets. There are a few important factors to consider.

What size will the pocket need to be? Keep in mind the soil will weigh more when wet. The size of the plant selected for the pocket is also a consideration. The bigger the plant, the more the sturdiness of the pocket becomes an crucial factor. Another important aspect is the composition of the wall or fence, as well as its placement in the garden. Will the wall pocket be in the path of strong winds? Will the plant material bake in the strong summer sun? Selecting the right site is important.

If the fence is wooden, installing a cross bar will add necessary support to compensate for the weight of the soil-filled pocket or bag. Mark the area to accommodate the size of the pocket on the fence. Center a 1- x 2-inch (2.5 x 5 cm) treated piece of lumber and secure it with wood screws. This support bracket also helps keep the planting pocket from resting directly on the fence. Once the support bracket is in place, measure and mark where the hooks will be installed. Drill a hole and screw the hooks into the support board.

If mounting a planting pocket on a masonry wall, you will need a drill, masonry drill bit, plastic anchors, and masonry hooks with a screw end. It is quite important to measure twice and mark once when drilling into hard surfaces of any type. Drill into the correctly marked spaces and gently tap the plastic anchors into place. Screw the hooks into the anchors and hang the wall pocket planter.

Planting pockets on a wall do not have to be a separate entity from the fence. If using small plants like herbs or succulents with shallow roots, creating a planting pocket can be quite simple. You will need two squares or rectangles of weed-blocking fabric or felt. One piece should be 1 inch (2.5 cm) larger than the other and a matching section of recycled plastic. You also need a handful of nails. Once again, site the pocket where it can easily be accessed for planting, as well as watering. Lay the recycled plastic over the smaller piece of weed block or felt. This will form the back of the planting pocket. The plastic lining will protect the wood from rotting behind the pocket. On the larger piece of felt or weed block, turn in the edges ¾ inch (1 cm) on three sides. Lay the smaller, plastic-lined piece under the folded edges. Using the nails, secure this pocket to the wall on three sides and plant. These pockets will generally last one to two seasons.

Extend the garden to include walls and fences by creating planting pockets for a pop of unexpected color, a collection of mini plants, or simply to try something new.

Stacked Planters

Planting up does not always mean growing on a trellis. Try planting in stacking containers. The options for pre-formed stacking planters has increased each year. There are some planters that are specifically made for stacking. These planters usually have three or four wells or pockets that interlock. Stacking them three or four high will take up less space than eight or twelve traditional small pots.

An additional benefit of a stacked planter is the versatility it provides. Changing the contents throughout the season or when the seasons change encourages gardeners to try new plants in a variety of plant combinations. These planters offer the gardener the option of stacking two on top of each other. This will form a low planting within or at the edge of a garden. Stacking more than two or three adds height inside of a garden bed, on a terrace, or even as a standalone focal point planter.

There are also steel rods that can be threaded through angled pots and offer a completely different look. Some of these planters are directly above each other, while others tilt away, allowing plants to spill over the edges of the pots. These structures can form a fountain-like effect of plants. The options of what to plant in them is endless. Consider creating an herb tower, or even a mixed planting of dwarf vegetables. Placing a stacked planter filled with rosemary or other assorted herbs near the kitchen door encourages harvesting and drying for later use. Having herbs within easy reach to harvest for grilling is a terrific idea. Think about placing a stacking planter filled with fragrant plants near a seating area. Imagine the scent that will be at nose level. Consider using scented geraniums, alyssum, or heliotrope for a fragrant stacking planter.

If you are feeling creative, try building a stacked planter by using cinder (cement) blocks or even bricks. You will also need scissors, weed-block fabric remnants, and potting soil. Determine the ultimate height of the stacking feature before you start. Lay the blocks or bricks to the desired length of the stacking planter. Begin stacking by staggering the brick or blocks creating planting pockets along the way. Place the weed-block remnants inside the pockets prior to planting or insert small pots. Planting in these pockets offers unimaginable options. Consider using low-growing or tailing succulents. As they cascade down or over the pocket, a simple stacked planter becomes a work of art. Painting prior to planting will also add a bit of whimsy to the stacked planter.

A creative stacked planter used as a low wall is a unique way to add additional seating. Using staggered masonry blocks, alternate solid sides with open hollow spaces on top or even on the front of the seating area. Using plants that require minimal water, fill some of the open hollow spaces to soften the edges and perhaps add a splash of color. Center cushions on the solid portion of the stacked planter to invite guests to sit comfortably, as the plants happily grow below. This is a great place to plant assorted edible plants, like mints to nibble on in the garden.

Stacked planters add many possibilities of raising the level of beautiful combinations in the garden.

About the Authors

Photo by Zoe Zindash

Photo by Kizi N'Kodia

Kathy Jentz is editor and publisher of *Washington Gardener Magazine* and hosts the popular GardenDC Podcast. She is also the editor of the *Water Garden Journal*, for the International Waterlily and Water Gardening Society; *The Azalean*, for the Azalea Society of Amerca; and *Fanfare*, for Region 3 of the American Daylily Society. Her mission is to turn black thumbs green. A life-long gardener, Kathy believes that growing plants should be stress-free and enjoyable. Her philosophy is inspiration over perspiration.

Teri Speight is a proud native Washingtonian. She is the former head gardener for the city of Fredericksburg, Virginia, one of the founding farmers of the Eitt CSA, Stafford County's first transitional organic CSA farm. Teri is currently an estate gardener, speaker, writer, and podcaster. She also serves on the National Garden Club board focusing on urban gardening. In 2020, she founded Jabali Amani Garden Club, the first virtual African-American garden club. Her website, Cottage in the Court, offers curated garden experiences for small groups and one-on-one garden coaching, specializing in earth-friendly practices.

Photographers' Credits

Brie Arthur: 15, 21, 42 (bottom left)

Christina Salwitz: 42 (top), 88 (top), 134, 185

George Weigel: 26, 46 (top), 48, 60-61, 118, 200

Janet Davis: 3 (left), 16-17, 20, 30-31, 32-33, 34, 38, 54, 56, 71, 88 (bottom), 90-91, 93 (top), 101, 102 (bottom), 107, 115 (top), 132, 159 (bottom), 160, 182 (bottom), 195

Jessica Walliser: 49, 94, 102 (top)

Jim Charlier: 12, 98, 104-105, 120, 126-127, 140-141, 172

Kathy Jentz: 3 (right), 4-5, 6, 8, 10, 18, 28, 50, 64, 67, 78, 83, 84, 86, 112, 131, 136, 137, 139, 142-143, 144, 147, 149, 150, 153, 154, 156-157, 159 (top), 166, 167, 168, 175, 176-177, 178, 180, 188, 192-193, 196

Mark Turner: 37, 41, 44, 45, 57, 62, 93 (bottom right), 108, 115 (bottom), 163, 190

Martha Swiss: 182 (top)

Shutterstock: 1, 3 (middle two), 9, 23, 24, 29, 42 (bottom right), 46 (bottom), 53, 58, 65, 66, 68, 73, 74, 76, 77, 81, 82, 93 (bottom left), 95, 96-97, 111, 116, 119, 123, 124, 128, 135, 148, 164, 171, 181, 186, 189, 199, 202

Stephanie Frey - Shutterstock: 87

Index

More books from Cool Springs Press about **small-space and urban gardening**

Field Guide to Urban Gardening
978-0-76036-396-6

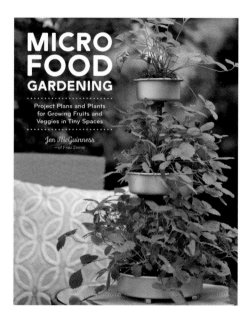

Micro Food Gardening
978-0-76036-983-8

Grow Bag Gardening
978-0-76036-868-8

Tiny Plants
978-0-76036-957-9